The Unfei

This book belongs to:

Ardell Winters
13612 Peach St
Southgate, MI 48195-1320

The Unfeigned
Love of God

Pastor Leonard Gardner

Edited by Brad Shirley

Cover Design: Chris Asimoudis

Visit www.booksurge.com to order additional copies.

The Unfeigned Love of God

CONTENTS

Chapter 1

Knowing the Unknowable

You may think that you have heard all there is to hear about love. You can hardly listen to a song or a sermon, or watch a movie or television show without hearing the word love mentioned, yet genuine love is not often demonstrated in the world around us. People have many definitions of love and many opinions about what love really is, but the only way to know true genuine love is to know the God who is love.

I believe that God wants us to understand His love for us in a new way, and He wants to bring us to a new level in His love. We have many ideas about love in our heads, but I am speaking of true heart change. I believe that there are some things that God is saying to His church that He wants us to hear.

In Ephesians 3:17-19, the Apostle Paul states, "That Christ may dwell in your hearts by faith; that you, being rooted and grounded in love, may be able to comprehend with all saints what is the breadth and length and depth and height." God has included _all_ believers in this! He wants us to comprehend "the breadth and length and depth and height and to know the love of Christ, which passeth knowledge, that ye might be filled with all the fullness of God."

Genuine Unfeigned Love

Both Peter (I Peter 1:22) and Paul (II Corinthians 6:4-6) used an adjective in their writings to describe the love of God.

The word that they chose, as they were directed by the Holy Spirit, was the word "unfeigned." They called the love of God "unfeigned love." The word "unfeigned" means "genuine, sincere, real, not pretentious, and not hypocritical." The word "genuine" refers to something whose characteristics and qualities are that of its author. Therefore, we can conclude that both Peter and Paul were saying that the love of God carries with it the character and the qualities of God. You can't separate *love* from *God*. God doesn't just love as an action. God *is* love. What comes out of God carries all the qualities and all the characteristics of everything that He is. It's not just a piece of Him or a part of Him. It's all that He is. Therefore, it follows that we really can't understand the love of God until we understand God Himself. God *is* love.

Sometimes when we speak about the love of God, we get uneasy because, deep within us, we feel unlovable and unlovely. We think, "How can God really love me? He knows all about me. He knows my weaknesses, my shortcomings, and my deepest struggles. How can He really love me? I am neither lovely nor loveable." Frequently, we strive to be perfect because we believe that God metes out His love based on our deservedness. Our human reasoning says that the more "perfect" we are, the more love of God we are entitled to receive.

To be sure, we need to live righteously. That is clear from Scripture. But even if you attain every goal and overcome every weakness, problem, failure, and inadequacy in your life, God will not love you any more than He loves you right now. Why? Because His love is awesome, perfect, and complete. His love lacks nothing. It isn't as if He gives you a piece of love and He gives someone else a bigger or smaller piece. He doesn't calculate how much love to give each person. When you receive His love, you receive it all.

Hard to Describe or Comprehend

In Ephesians 3:17-19, Paul was effectively saying, "I want you to know the height, depth, breadth, and length of this immeasurable love of God so that you won't need to have confirmation from people. You won't need to belong to cliques or compromise your beliefs to fit in and be accepted." He wrote in Ephesians 1:6, "You have been accepted in the beloved."

This can be difficult to comprehend because we are accustomed to people's love. People will fail you and hurt you. People will leave you in confusion and pain. Human love is shallow, fickle, and temporal, but human love is not like the love of God. Paul wrote in **Romans 8:38-39**, "I am persuaded that neither death, nor life, nor angels, nor principalities, nor powers, nor things present, nor things to come, nor height, nor depth, nor any other creature, shall be able to separate us from the love of God, which is in Christ Jesus our Lord." _Nothing_ can separate you from God's love.

Some years ago, someone wrote a song in which the composer endeavored to describe the love of God. The song said, "It's rich. It's pure. It's measureless. It's strong. It reaches beyond the beyond." But the composer ran out of words, because there isn't a big enough dictionary to describe the love of God. You will quickly exhaust your vocabulary trying to describe it.

Logos and Rhema

In Ephesians 3:17-19, Paul was saying, "I want you to be able to comprehend this love. I want you to know something that can't be known." That sounds contradictory or paradoxical. What is God trying to say to us? How can we know something that is beyond knowledge? As we study this passage carefully we find that Paul is really saying "I want you to progressively experience something that is beyond the information that you can put in your head. I want you to come into something that is beyond what you can comprehend with your human mind. I want to take the _logos_, the Word of God—the principles, concepts, and unapplied truth—and make it _rhema_ to you." The Greek word _rhema_ means "alive, relevant, and vital in your current situation and circumstances." The Greek word _logos_ means "the whole of the Word of God, the 'big picture' Word." We have a lot of _logos_ in our minds. We know it and we can quote it, but Paul is saying it is God's will to take us to a higher level. God does that in one of two ways. One way is by "revelation" and the other is by "progressive experience." God says, "I will take you through some experiences, and you will come out of these experiences at a higher level, and this *logos* is going to become *rhema* to you." When *logos* becomes *rhema,* no one can take it away from you or tear it from your heart. It becomes absolute, relevant, living, powerful truth to you, and not simply something you learned from a classroom, a tape, a book, a sermon, or a teaching. We have heard a lot of teaching and many sermons. Thank God for the declaration of the Word and the truth that has come forth. But what God is interested in, in each of our lives, is bringing us to a level where we possess living, relevant, powerful truth that revitalizes us, drives us, challenges us, gives us vision, and gives us anointing and purpose.

The living Word of God is spirit, and it is life. It becomes so real and alive to you that it ceases to be a matter of debate or argument. You simply "know that you know." Once in a while, your head might say "I don't understand," but your heart says "Don't worry about it. I know that I know." You don't bring it up for a vote every morning. It has become alive, real, powerful, and life-changing inside of you.

Abraham's Example

The Bible declares that God called Abraham His friend, and He made covenant with him. God said, "Come out of your country, and I will take you to a new place. I will take you to a new level, and I will show you some things that you have never seen or known before." Abraham said, "All right, God. I don't know where we are going or what this is all about, but I am going with you." If God were to explain the plan of redemption to His friend Abraham, He might have said something like, "Abraham, the world is full of sin and there must be a remedy. I am going to send My only begotten Son to the earth. He will be conceived of the Holy Spirit and born of a virgin. He will live a sinless life, and I will put all the sins of the world on Him. He will die on a cross and become the sacrifice for the sins of all humanity. He will rise again and bring new life to those who repent, believe, and receive Him." Abraham may have said, "I understand. I believe You, God."

But God did more than that. He took Abraham through an incredible "hands on" life lesson about sacrifice (Genesis 22:1-14). He said, "Abraham, this is not just going to be information. I am going to make it so real that you will never doubt. Abraham, take your only son Isaac to the mountain, build an altar, put wood on it, lay your son on that altar, and offer him up to Me." That was more than a Sunday school lesson. I can imagine Abraham walking up that mountain saying, "Isaac, I really love you. You are the son of promise. You mean everything to me." Abraham's head must have been spinning, and his heart must have been in his throat, but he built the altar, stacked the wood, and raised the knife. At that moment, God said, "Abraham, wait. I have provided a sacrifice." Abraham looked up and he saw the sacrifice that God provided—a ram caught in a thicket. Abraham sacrificed the ram, and Isaac was spared. God had walked Abraham through an experience that brought a real revelation and an understanding of redemption like he would have never learned through words alone. I am not against tapes, books, sermons, or teachings, but God wants to bring us to a level where the *rhema* of God is so alive in us that we are "on fire" for God and we are walking in the fullness of the truth.

Many times people that have walked through hard places and faced impossible situations, as Abraham did, have come out with a *rhema* from God that causes them to never be the same again. Some may say, "Do I *have* to go through those things to get there?" I don't think so. I believe God can give revelation apart from experience that in some instances will spare us from difficult times. But in other cases, He walks us through challenges, and when we get through them, we "know that we know" and nobody can take it from us. It becomes so alive in us that everyone we touch is affected by it.

God said, "I want to show My love to My people. I want them to understand it." I firmly believe that we will not see the fullness of the harvest that God wants to bring in until we come into a complete understanding of the love of God.

The Story of Hosea and Gomer

In 785 BC, God reached out to a man named Hosea, who was of the tribe of Issachar and a native of the northern kingdom. His story can be found in the book of Hosea. God put His hand on Hosea to teach him the love of God through experience, and He recorded it so that we would have the benefit of it and be blessed by it. We can be changed and affected by it because we can see the love of God in action. As I tell Hosea's story over the course of the next few pages, please allow me some poetic license as I imagine what Hosea must have thought and felt, and as I tell this story by paraphrasing the Word of God.

Hosea was a very Godly young man, a prophet by calling. God spoke to him and said, "Hosea, I have prepared you for this time in your life. It is now time for you to be married." That is an exciting time in any young man's life. Hosea might have said, "Thank you, Lord. I have been waiting for this! Can You tell me who the special girl is?"

Hosea must have been shocked when God told him to marry a prostitute named Gomer. "Her? She is the one that You have chosen to be my wife? What will my friends say? Lord, my prophet buddies all married girls that sing in the choir, play the piano, and teach Sunday school. Are You sure about this, God?" A miracle happened in Hosea's heart, and the miracle was not that he married Gomer. In marrying her, Hosea was simply being obedient to God. The miracle was that he actually loved her. All of a sudden, something happened in his heart and he felt an attraction and a deep love for her. "God, I can't seem to get her off my mind. I think about her night and day. What has happened to me, God? I love her."

The word "Gomer" means "complete." Gomer had never been complete, even though that is what her name meant. The word "Hosea," means 'deliverance' and 'salvation.' Salvation, as interpreted in Scripture by the Greek words *sozo* and *soteria,* includes deliverance and healing. It implies wholeness; all the provision of God for the whole person. Hosea ("deliverance") had come into Gomer's life to make her complete. Hosea came to make her what she had always been called ("complete"), yet had never been. Though her name had been "complete," she had always been incomplete. Through this story, I believe God is showing us how painful, difficult, and uncomfortable it is to love some people. When you know that you are really in love, you cease to care what your friends say. "I love her, and I don't care what anyone else thinks. God, is this how You feel about me? Is this how You feel about Your people? Is this what is going on in Your heart, God, this compelling, driving force to look at our ugliness and our dirtiness, and still be committed to bring us to wholeness and completion? Is this what You are teaching us, God?" Hosea took Gomer to his home, married her, cleaned her up, and gave her some new clothes. He took her to church, and he taught her how to "do church:" how to clap her hands, how to smile, how to say "Praise the Lord," and how to put her arm around someone and say "I am with you, hang in there."

Gomer's Unfaithfulness and Hosea's Love

But Gomer had a problem, because deep down inside her there was a conflict. She was going through all of the outward motions, but her heart wasn't in it. There was a war going on inside. She was now different on the outside, but she was still struggling on the inside. She tried her best. She tried to learn how to wash and iron clothes and clean the house. She never had a house before. Through it all, she had a horrible hidden pain in her heart. She was saying to herself, "Hosea doesn't know who I really am. He doesn't understand the real me." She started to disappear from home for periods of time. She would eventually come back with some weak excuse, and she would try hard again for awhile, but this struggle was still going on inside of her.

Despite her infidelity, Hosea continued to love Gomer. Hosea was walking through something that was deeply painful, yet he remained faithful. The day came that Gomer went away and didn't come back. Hosea was left to take care of the house, wash the clothes, cook the meals, and care for the kids. The toughest thing about it was that the kids didn't even look like him! The Bible states that they were children of her wanderings. Hosea was taking care of children that weren't his.

The love of God is so great that God takes care of many things in our life that He never birthed. We have birthed some "Ishmaels," things that God never intended for us. We deserve punishment, but instead He continues to love us and He takes care of things because He is a good God. He takes care of things that He never set in motion. We come up with plans and programs that God never ordained. The cry of my heart is that I will not birth any Ishmaels.

Gomer was gone a long time, and Hosea said to himself, "She has been gone before, but never this long." Perhaps as you read this, you are someone that has been "gone too long." Perhaps someone hurt you or said something they shouldn't have said. Perhaps you didn't like what happened or what someone did to you. If you have been gone too long, come back to the Lord. He loves you and is awaiting your return.

The Search and the Redemption

Hosea started looking out the window, like the father of the prodigal son, waiting for Gomer to come back. When is she going to come back home? When is she going to come back to "deliverance?" She didn't come back, so he thought, "I am going to go and find her, because I love her." He searched the streets and went to the places that she used to go, but she wasn't there. As he was looking for her, he heard a noise down the street. It sounded like an auction. "Surely she will not be there. They probably have some pottery, jewelry, and a few slaves that they are auctioning off. No, she would not be there." He kept searching, but he couldn't find her. "Where is she? Where is the one I love?" Finally he thought, "I have looked everywhere else, so I will go over there and look at the slave auction." He went, and to his amazement, he saw her there.

"Gomer, what are you doing on the slave table? You are dirty, your hair is matted, and your clothing is torn. What are you doing here, Gomer? You have a home. You have someone that loves you." He turned to a bidder nearby and said, "So you want to buy her? No way. You are not going to have her. She is mine. You cannot buy her. You have hurt her enough. You have looked upon her as a piece of property. *She is my wife.* I am going to buy her. I will pay whatever it costs. There is no price too great. I need her. I want her. Fifteen pieces of silver? Okay. One and a half homers of barley? Okay." Silver symbolizes redemption in Scripture. Jesus was sold for thirty pieces of silver when he was betrayed by someone He loved. Hosea said, "I want her. Here is everything I have. Take it. I will pour it all out. I want her. I love her. She is my wife. She can't belong to another. I know she is dirty. I know she is messed up. I know that she walked away from what she could have had. I know, but I love her anyway. Tell her I am coming to get her because I love her."

Hosea paid the price for Gomer. He gave everything he had. It's embarrassing to have to buy back what you already own, but that is precisely what *redeem* means. *Redeem* means "to buy back, to re-purchase what was already yours." It is difficult to understand that kind of genuine love, but God is showing us what redemption really means, and what His love really does. Hosea said, "Gomer, come back home. I am going to restore everything to you. I am going to give you what your heart desires because I love you, Gomer. I know you don't look like much. I know you are dirty, your hair is matted, and your clothes are torn. I know that you have been beaten, abused, and treated badly. I know that you are messed up. You have made mistakes, Gomer, but I love you. I don't love you because you are beautiful. I don't love you only when your hair is fixed. I love you because you are mine." Dear God, please help us to understand this powerful truth.

Restoration!

Some of the most powerful words in the Bible are found in Hosea 2:15-16, which effectively states, "I am going to give you your joy back. I am going to give you the vineyards. That is where the grapes grow, where the juice comes from. That is where the joy flows. I am going to give you glory. I am not here to beat you down or punish you. I am not here to give what you deserve. I am here to love you, and I am going to restore everything unto you." Gomer looked at Hosea and she said, "Okay, master." The Hebrew word for master is "Baali." "Okay, Baali, you bought me fair and square. You paid the price. You did what had to be done. You ignored my filthiness and opened your heart to me as a person. Baali, you can be my master, and the rest of my life I will be your slave."

Hosea 2:16 gives us the beautiful ending to this story, "And it shall be at that day, saith the Lord, thou shalt call Me Ishi." In Hebrew that means "husband." Hosea said, "You are not going to be my slave. I didn't seek you out to enslave you. I sought you out to deliver you. My name is 'deliverance.' I have come to make you complete. No, our relationship is not going to be Baali; it is going to be Ishi." Hosea didn't say, "Come home, *slave*." He said, "Come home, <u>*wife*</u>. I love you. You have been gone too long, but you are worth everything I have."

I believe that when all was said and done, Hosea had an understanding of the love of God that he could not have obtained any other way. After his experience, redemptive love became more than just a phrase or a concept that someone told him about. He felt the pain, the hurt, the breaking, and the cost. God said, "Write down your story because My church needs to understand My love." How quickly we reject and deny people! How quickly we disqualify them because they don't look like us, think like us, act like us, or believe like us. But God said, "Go out into the highways and byways and compel them to come in." He said, "Get the lame, the ones that don't walk right. Get the blind, the ones that can't see right. Get the deaf, the ones that can't hear right. Get them all. There is room at My table. It's time for them to come home. I don't care where they are coming from. I don't care about the color of their skin or their background. Just tell them I love them, and I paid the price for them." Hosea had come into a *rhema* understanding of the unfeigned love of God.

Chapter 2

Love Envieth Not

In his famous discourse on genuine love in I Corinthians 13, the Apostle Paul wrote that "Love envieth not." True genuine unfeigned Godly love does not have even a trace of envy in it. In this chapter, we will examine envy, and we will see in Scripture an excellent example of a man, John the Baptist, who exemplified the unfeigned love of God.

John 3:22 declares, "After these things came Jesus and His disciples into the land of Judea, and there He tarried with them and baptized." John 4:2 states that it wasn't Jesus, but rather His disciples, which did the baptizing. He was there with them, and they began to baptize.

John 3:23-26 states, "And John also was baptizing in Aenon near to Salim because there was much water there, and they came and were baptized, for John was not yet cast into prison. Then there arose a question between some of John's disciples and the Jews about purifying. And they <the disciples of John> came unto John and said unto him, Rabbi, He that was with thee beyond Jordan, to whom thou barest witness, behold the same baptizeth and all men come to Him." Please note that it states that _all men_ were coming to Him.

John 3:27-30 continues, "John answered and said, A man can receive nothing except it be given him from heaven. Ye yourselves bear me witness that I said I am not the Christ but that I am sent before Him. He that hath the bride is the bridegroom, but the friend of the bridegroom, which standeth and heareth him, rejoiceth greatly because of the bridegroom's voice. Thus my joy therefore is fulfilled. He must increase but I must decrease."

John the Baptist and Jesus

It was very early in the first year of Jesus' earthly ministry, and this was the first ministry trip Jesus had taken into Judea. He had already turned water into wine in Cana of Galilee. He had already spoken to Nicodemus about being born again. He had already healed many who were sick and set many captives free. Here, not far from Jerusalem, He and His disciples began to minister to the people. He authorized His disciples to baptize the people that came to Him there. John the Baptist was also baptizing, but he was baptizing about seventy-five to ninety miles northeast of where Jesus was. John was on the west side of the Jordan River in an area known as Samaria, and he was continuing his dynamic and powerful ministry of baptizing the many people that had come to him.

One day, John's disciples came to him very upset and said, "John, we just encountered something that really troubles us. We were down in Judea, and there is a man baptizing many people. He is the one that you introduced to us on the other side of the Jordan, when you pointed to Him and you said, 'Behold the Lamb of God that taketh away the sins of the world.' John, this troubles us because everyone is going to Him." John's disciples were troubled because they perceived John was losing popularity, that he was losing his number one status as the baptizer. "John, how can this be? Baptism is *our* ministry. What is He doing with our ministry? You introduced Him and now He is taking over." John must have thought, "Why are they so upset because Jesus is baptizing and people are going to Him instead of me?" I believe that John's disciples were struggling with what sports psychiatrists call "reflected glory." It was very important to them that John be the "top dog," because if you can't be the top dog yourself, you want to be associated with the one that is the top dog. If the one you are associated with is "slipping in the ratings," it has a negative effect on your self-esteem and your pride. They were troubled about what was happening.

Many people today are rabid sports fans. Their mood and emotions rise and fall with the success or failure of their favorite team. If their team wins, they are on an emotional high, and if their team loses, they are depressed. This is called "reflected glory." A psychiatrist at the University of Utah did some research, and he claimed that the testosterone levels in men that are avid sports fans increase twenty percent when their team is winning and decrease twenty percent when their team is losing.

I believe that John's disciples were struggling with "reflected glory" issues. I am certain that the enemy wanted to abort John's ministry, and perhaps he tried to get John to think, "If Jesus is doing better than I am, perhaps I should modify my ministry." Perhaps one of his disciples even had some suggestions. "John, you must modify your message if you want more people to come. I have heard that many people aren't happy about the repentance message that you have been preaching. Remember that sermon you preached entitled 'Generation of Vipers'? People didn't react favorably to it. John, you should dress a little better and mind your manners. It's not attractive when grasshoppers are hanging out of your mouth. John, we must do something about your public image. If we don't do something, even more people will be leaving us and flocking to Jesus."

Perhaps John was tempted to consider Jesus as a competitor and to get angry at Him. It is possible that the enemy was out to subtly strip the ministry from John. I am grateful that John did not yield to any of those apparent temptations. He didn't modify his message. There is no evidence he changed his dress. There is absolutely no proof that he ever opposed Jesus or considered Him an enemy. John simply kept doing what God had called him to do. He continued to be what God had told him to be, and God was able to continue to use him in a very unique ministry. As I consider the whole scenario that is outlined here, I am certain that the enemy had a desire to trap John in what Scripture calls "envy."

Envy

What is envy? Envy is the desire to have something that someone else has, and the accompanying bad feeling because you don't have it. Envy is to be frustrated by God's goodness to someone else, while denying or taking for granted God's goodness to you. Envy causes us to mourn when others rejoice and to rejoice when others mourn. Envy wants everyone else to be as unsuccessful as you feel.

Envy is prominent throughout the Scriptures. It is found in the stories of Cain and Abel, Ishmael and Isaac, Joseph and his brothers, Miriam and Aaron, Leah and Rachel, and Ahab and Naboth. Envy attempted to prevent Jesus' birth and dogged Him all the way through His earthly ministry. Envy even delivered Jesus up to His death (Matthew 27:18). Envy is one of the most devious and destructive devices of Satan, and he works it in the human heart whenever he can. Galatians 5:29 names envy as one of the works of the flesh. We shudder at the words "cancer" and "AIDS." We should shudder at the word "envy," because it imprisons, poisons, and destroys. It will destroy your heart and your purpose if you allow it into your life.

How can we overcome envy? The answer is in I Corinthians 13:4, which declares, "Charity <love> envieth not." The Greek word *agape* (the unconditional, pure, God kind of love) is translated "charity" in that verse. In other words, the unfeigned love of God is absolutely void of any evidence of envy.

John the Baptist stood up against the temptation to be envious and he overcame it, and his ministry continued on as strong as ever. The beautiful thing about *agape* is that, according to Romans 5:5, "It is shed abroad in our hearts by the Holy Spirit." Within our veil of flesh, there is the seed of the love of God. The *agape* dwells in each of us who are born again. If *agape* love is allowed to be released, it will overcome and overwhelm the feelings, emotions, demands, and desires of the flesh.

I believe that John the Baptist exhibited three principles which demonstrate that he was walking in the *agape* love of God and had no envy in his heart. If we understand and embrace these three principles that he exemplified, we will overcome envy as John did.

Principle #1 — Know You Are Chosen

First of all, I believe that John *knew that he was chosen.* In John 3:27, John's answer to his disciples was "A man can receive nothing except it be given him from heaven." John basically looked at his disciples, and said, "Guys, there is no problem. You are upset about what is going on in Judea, but Jesus couldn't be doing what He is doing if the Father didn't give that ministry to Him. Because the Father gave it to Him doesn't mean that He took anything away from me." Envy is the poison in the hearts of people that feel "unchosen." John understood that the choosing of Jesus did not mean the rejection of John.

The devil is a master of contention, strife, and jealousy. We have all felt envious at one time or another, but we can only overcome envy when we begin to live in the truth that we were chosen of God. When you get that in your spirit, it will release you from experiencing unnecessary pain. In John 15:16, Jesus said, "You have not chosen Me. I have chosen you." He went on to say in John 15:19, "I have chosen you out of the world." I Peter 2:9 states, "You are a chosen generation." Ephesians 1:4 declares, "You were chosen in Him before the foundation of the world." If you settle that in your heart, it will set you free. There is no pain quite like the pain of rejection, but to be *chosen* translates into being *loved.*

I remember reading a story of a little girl who spoke of how she had felt unloved her whole life. She was born with a cleft palate, and her appearance was marred to the point that her mouth was twisted, her teeth and her nose were crooked, and her speech was garbled. People made fun of her, and the pain was so great that, when people would ask her what was wrong, she found that it was less painful to tell people that it happened as a result of an accident rather than telling them that she had been born that way. She said, "I got to the place that I believed the only people that could ever love me were my family members. They were the only ones who could really love me the way I was." She went on to tell about the experience that changed her life. She said, "When I was in the second grade, I had a teacher by the name of Mrs. Leonard. One day, she was giving us our hearing tests." She would take the students one by one and stand them against the door and then whisper something, and if they could whisper the same words back, it was satisfactory proof that their hearing was acceptable. And so she went down through the class, and, she would say things like "The sky is blue" or "You have new shoes," and the student would whisper it back. Finally it was this girl's turn. The teacher stood the little girl up against the door, covered her one ear, and said in whispered tones, "I wish you were my little girl." She said, "It changed my life. Someone wanted me. I was chosen. I was special." To be chosen means three things. It means that you are unique, that you have something to give, and that someone wants you.

The world mistakenly believes that when one person is chosen, someone else is being rejected. When one person asks another to marry them, someone else is not chosen. When you are given the job, someone else isn't given the job. When a young woman is crowned Miss America, many others are rejected. But in God, that is not true. When we are chosen in God, it is not at someone else's expense. My choosing doesn't mean your rejection, nor does your choosing mean my rejection. I am enhanced when you are chosen, and you are enhanced when I am chosen. If you understand this, it will set you free, because you may feel rejected. You may feel "unchosen." You may have been told by parents or others that you are no good, you can't make it, and you are not worth anything. That is a lie. You may feel rejected because you didn't get the job, the guy or girl, or the promotion, but please know that you are unique to God. You have something to give. He loves you, and He made you just like you are. You are chosen by God.

John understood this truth. He didn't have to modify his message, change his clothes, or be concerned about the number of people that were following Jesus instead of him. He said, "Jesus wouldn't have anything if the Father didn't give it to Him.

But because the Father also gave a baptizing ministry to Him doesn't take anything away from mine. The kingdom of God is stronger now. The kingdom of God is more powerful now. The kingdom of God has been enhanced. Let us rejoice." I believe John saw something that God wants us to see. Sometimes, in our feelings of failure and weakness, we don't feel that we deserve to be loved or chosen, and so we struggle. God wants you to know that He made you and He chose you. You are unique. You are not just another brick in the wall. You are not just a number. You are you, and you are special. Before the foundations of the world were made, He knew that He would make *you*.

We hear the phrase "God loves everyone equally," but I would like to correct that, because sometimes equally is not enough. As a child in a large family, even though you are told you are loved equally along with your brothers and sisters, sometimes that is not enough. God loves you *uniquely*. That is a different word than *equally*. He loves you for you. You are unique and special. He loves you uniquely, and He loves the person next to you uniquely, and He loves the next one uniquely. There is simply a unique love that He has for you. You don't have to become like someone else. Just be you. He loves you. You are the way He wants you to be. John rejected the temptation to be envious of Jesus because John was secure in the fact that he was chosen and God loved him.

Principle #2 — Know Your Place

A second thing John said is found in John 3:28, "Ye yourselves bear me witness that I said I am not the Christ but I am sent before Him." There are two key phrases there. One phrase is "I am not," and the other phrase is "I am." I believe it is extremely important to know *who you are*, and *who you are not*. You must know your place. Some people continually try to be who they are not, and in doing so, they are not being who they really are. John said, "Look, disciples, let me get something straight. I know who I am not, and I don't have a problem with that. I don't have a problem with Jesus getting bigger crowds than I do."

For a number of years in ministry, I wanted so badly to sing. I kept trying to sing, but it took me a long time to realize that I am not a singer. Thank the Lord that He raised up my children who can sing. Our church didn't start growing until I stopped singing. You can relax in what you are if you know what you are not. You don't have to keep striving, worrying, and working to be what you are not. Let us make this Christian journey exciting and wonderful and joyful and glorious and be what we are.

The next verse amplifies this truth. John said, "He that hath the bride is the bridegroom." He was speaking of himself when he said, "The friend of the bridegroom, which standeth and heareth him, he rejoiceth greatly because of the bridegroom's voice. Thus my joy therefore is fulfilled." John was saying, "I get joy from being what I know that I am supposed to be." He said to his disciples, "You must understand something. I am not the bridegroom. Jesus is the bridegroom. I am just the friend of the bridegroom." The word that was given to that role in ancient Jewish weddings was the word "*shoshbin.*"

John said, "I am the *shoshbin.* Jesus is the bridegroom." The *shoshbin*, by definition, is very much like the "best man" in our western culture, and he had three primary responsibilities. Number one, he sent out the invitations to the wedding. John had been preaching, "Prepare ye the way of the Lord. Make his path straight." He was, in effect, inviting people to Jesus' "party." Number two, the *shoshbin* accompanied the bridegroom to the wedding. Number three, and most important of all, the *shoshbin* was responsible, on the last night of the seven day wedding feast, to stand outside the tent where the bride was waiting for her bridegroom. In the darkness of the night, the bride would be taken into the tent waiting for her bridegroom to come and claim her, and in order to protect her and to prepare her, the *shoshbin* was to stand outside the tent and make sure that no one went into the tent. When he heard the voice of the bridegroom, he would simply step aside and let the bridegroom go in and claim his bride with joy.

The *shoshbin* knew that his job wasn't to claim the bride; his job was to protect the bride until the bridegroom came for her. The bridegroom had a special joy in claiming his bride, and that joy belonged to the bridegroom alone. John said, "I am the *shoshbin*. My joy is found in being the friend of the bridegroom. There is a special joy in my place, my calling, and my responsibility. I am not going to try to get joy from what someone else is called to do. I find real joy in doing what I am called to do." The devil wasn't able to make John envious. John said, "I don't have any problem with Jesus. I am just waiting for His voice, and when I hear it, I am going to step aside. He deserves to be on center stage. I have only been here preparing the way. I am His friend."

I believe there is a reason that Jesus said in Matthew 11:11 that of all those born of women, John the Baptist rose to be the greatest. The word "rose" is *yergo* in the Greek language. It means "to come to a higher level." John had come to a higher place of understanding. He knew that there was no need for contention or competition. I personally know, as a minister and a longtime pastor, that I am a *shoshbin*. I have the privilege of doing my best to feed, encourage, lead, and inspire people that Jesus places in my care. I know that no one belongs to me. They belong to Jesus. They are His bride. There is a joy in knowing that and fulfilling my purpose. John said, "I have the joy of the friend of the bridegroom." And he said, "You are not going to take my joy from me." He knew his place.

Principle #3—Learn to Let Go...and Trust

In John 3:30, John the Baptist said, "He must increase, but I must decrease." He was saying, "I have learned how to let go." When you know you are chosen and loved, and you know that you have a place, then you can let go. Sometimes the things that we are trying to hold onto will prevent us from going to the next level. We must learn to let go. Parents have to learn to "let go" of their children when they start going to school, when they start learning how to drive, and when they go off to college. It is very hard to do so, but it is important. There is a story of a man that fell off a cliff, and as he fell toward certain death, he reached out his hand in desperation and grabbed a limb, and he hung there.

He looked up to the top of the cliff, and he saw that there was no way to climb up. He looked down, and he saw that it was a very long drop to the ground below. He hung onto that limb, looked up and said, "Is anybody up there?" A voice came back and said, "Yes. I am God, and I am going to save you." The man said, "Wonderful! What should I do?" God said, "Let go." The man said, "Is anybody else up there?"

It is called trust. We don't know what tomorrow is going to bring. We don't know what the future holds. We must learn to trust. John had learned throughout his life when to hold on and when to let go. He had learned to _hold on_ to his faith, his message, and his calling, in spite of all the ridicule and persecution. He had learned to _let go_ of a lot of things that the flesh wants to hang on to, such as living a normal life, having a normal job, and accumulating worldly possessions. Having let go of all of those things, he was now being asked to let go of his ministry. That might have been the toughest thing of all to let go of, but he did it. "Jesus must increase, and I must decrease."

Did you ever wonder why December 25 has been chosen to celebrate Christmas? Jesus was not born on that day. I believe one of the reasons that December 25th was chosen is because it is at that time of the year when we have the shortest days, and darkness begins giving way to light. At that time, we are starting to gain minutes of daylight each and every day. It is symbolic of Christ's coming. John 1:4-5 declares, "In Him was life, and the life was the light of men, and the light shineth in darkness, and the darkness comprehendeth it not." December is the time of the year when the positioning of our earth and the sun are such that the days begin to grow longer. Darkness begins to be swallowed up by light. Do you know what day on the religious calendar is celebrated as John the Baptist's birthday? It is June 24th, because it's near the longest day of the year, and it is that time of the year when the light begins to give way to darkness. John said, "I must decrease. My work is finished. My course has been run, but the light and glory of the Son of God will shine forever."

In this short Bible passage about John the Baptist, God has unveiled a truth to us that is intended to set us free. God is saying, "Here is a secret I want you to embrace. Here is a truth I want you to internalize. Here is something that will set you free. When the devil comes knocking on the door of your heart, when he attacks your mind and you feel like you are losing it, when you are tossing and turning and you can't sleep or seem to think clearly, take hold of this truth. This will liberate you. This will set you free."

Remember the three principles we have learned here. Repeat them to yourself.

1) I have been chosen.

2) I have a place.

3) I can let go, because I can trust.

I believe that God is preparing us to go to a higher level. We speak of the importance of unity, and we all know it's important, but we must start dealing with the things that prevent unity. God is showing us how to deal with these things of the flesh, of the Adam nature, which cause all of the divisions between the Esaus and the Jacobs, the Cains and the Abels, the Josephs and his brothers, the Ishmaels and the Isaacs, the Rachels and the Leahs, and the Ahabs and the Naboths. Dear Lord, help us to overcome envy in our lives. May that unfeigned love which You have shed abroad in our hearts set us free.

Chapter 3

Where Art Thou?

It was the last time Jesus would pass through Jericho before He went to Calvary. Jericho was a very prosperous city which was often referred to as a city of sin and gross darkness, yet Jesus didn't exclude Jericho from His plan and His journey. There was a man named Zaccheus in Jericho whose encounter with Jesus reveals to us another dimension and expression of the unfeigned love of God.

Luke 19, starting in verse 1, states, "And Jesus entered and passed through Jericho. And, behold, there was a man named Zaccheus, which was the chief among the publicans, and he was rich. And he sought to see Jesus who He was, and could not for the press, because he was little of stature. And he ran before and climbed up into a sycamore tree to see Him, for He, Jesus, was to pass that way. And when Jesus came to the place, He looked up and saw him and said unto him, Zaccheus, make haste, come down, for today I must abide at thy house. And he made haste and came down and received Him joyfully. And when they saw it"—that is, the people that were standing there with Him, some religious leaders, some disciples—"when they saw it, they all murmured, saying that He was gone to be guest with a man that is a sinner. And Zaccheus stood and said unto the Lord, Behold, Lord, the half of my goods I give to the poor, and if I have taken anything from any man by false accusation, I restore him fourfold. And Jesus said unto him, This day is salvation come to this house, for as much as he also is a son of Abraham."

Verse 10 declares, "For the Son of Man is come to seek and to save that which was lost."

Despised Occupations

In Israel, during the time of the earthly ministry of Jesus, there were a number of vocations that were identified by the religious leaders as undesirable, and many of the young men were instructed not to pursue these professions because these occupations were so dishonorable and unethical. In fact, the religious leaders grouped the undesirable professions into three categories. One category was called the "despised" occupations. Two of the occupations on the list of the despised were the physician and the butcher. They were called "despised" because these occupations gave special attention to the rich and ignored the poor, so they were felt to be unjust and unfair. There is absolutely nothing inherently wrong with the occupation of physician or butcher. Thank God for good and Godly physicians. Luke himself, the author of the books of Luke and Acts, was a physician. He traveled with Paul. There is nothing wrong with the occupation itself as long as it is practiced justly and honestly, but young men were told not to pursue that profession because there was so much injustice and unfairness.

Dishonorable Occupations

A second category was called the "dishonorable" occupations. Among those particular occupations were the "tanner of dead animal skins," the "dung collector," and the "garbage collector." Young men were told, "Don't get involved in those occupations. They are unclean and dirty." There was even a legal provision which allowed a wife to divorce her husband if he was employed in one of these professions.

Immoral Occupations

A third category, and the one I will address in greater detail, was called the "immoral" occupations. These were not just dishonorable, not just despised, but immoral. There were four professions listed in this category, two of which involved gambling. The first was a person that gambled with dice. A second was a man that trained pigeons which were used for pigeon races, which men gambled on. A third was called the occupation of "usury," in which someone would loan money at high interest rates. It was considered immoral because most of the people that were involved in that practice took advantage of the poor. The fourth occupation that was considered immoral was the "tax collector." If you were a dung collector, a tanner, a gambler, a pigeon trainer, or someone in the profession of usury or tax collector, you were despised. It's interesting that such focus would be on the particular occupation of tax collector. It's also interesting how Jesus dealt with tax collectors during His earthly ministry, and how He did not exclude them from the plan and love of God.

The Tax Collector

The occupation of tax collector came about because much of Israel was occupied by the Romans at that time, and it was the desire of the Roman Empire to squeeze all of the money out of Israel that it could. They did it by any means, regardless of whether it was fair, legal, or just. Their whole system of taxation was corrupt. Rome delineated certain geographical regions, and then put the tax collection position for each region out for bids. The "bid" was the amount of money that the tax collector promised to collect for Rome. Anyone could bid to be the tax collector for a region. Sometimes the bidders were Romans, but frequently they were Jews. The highest bidder had to pay Rome the agreed upon price, but everything that he collected over and above that amount he kept for himself. As you can imagine, all kinds of scheming and evildoing came into practice.

Tax collectors came to be known as people that were out to steal from the people. They were considered thieves, and they would take everything they could from the people. The Jewish people considered them traitors because they sold themselves out morally to Rome and, in the name of greed, cheated their own families and neighbors. Anything was acceptable to them in the name of profit, so these people were absolutely despised.

It was commonly said in Israel that "repentance is very hard for a tax collector," and many people believed it was impossible. Certain political and social limitations were placed on tax collectors. For example, tax collectors were forbidden to be witnesses in a court of law because they were considered to be too dishonest. Secondly, they were forbidden to be judges because of the stigma associated with the occupation. Thirdly, very devout Jews would take great care that even the hem of their garments would not touch the hem of the garment of a tax collector. In general, people stayed away from tax collectors, considering them to be evil, corrupt traitors.

Zaccheus

In that context, the Holy Spirit takes the searchlight of heaven and shines it on a man who was not only a tax collector, but a *chief* tax collector. He was so good at his trade that he had responsibility over other tax collectors. He knew all the tricks of the trade, and he was apparently a good schemer. His name was Zaccheus. Obviously, his parents had no idea how he was going to turn out, because they named him Zaccheus, which means "pure and justified." As a tax collector, he was anything but pure and justified. We don't know much about him except for one physical characteristic that the Bible identifies. He was very short; what some might call "vertically challenged." That is all we really know about him, aside from the fact that he was a very successful tax collector. Evidently, as a young man, he had disregarded all of the recommendations of his elders and had gone into this very corrupt occupation. For the love of money, he became unconcerned about having close friends or being accepted by his neighbors or his family.

Jesus, the Son of God, the most pure, just, honest, and holy man that has ever lived, had no problem with tax collectors. In fact, He had already chosen one of them, a man named Matthew, to be part of His group. Jesus walked by the gate of the city one day, looked at Matthew (also called Levi), and said, "Follow Me. Don't lay down your pen. You can leave your books, but hang onto your pen because we are going to use that later. You are going to write a book for Me." Can you imagine what must have gone on among the group of disciples? They were very zealous. They were dedicated Israelites, and to accept Matthew into the group was not easy, because tax collectors were so despised. Jesus said, "I want you," and Matthew left everything to follow Him. Matthew was so excited about being chosen by Jesus that he threw a party for all his tax collector friends, and Jesus went to the party!

Through this, God is showing us a new dimension of His heart and His love. Jesus didn't seem to have any problem with those whom other people despised. Zaccheus heard that Jesus was going to pass through Jericho, and he was curious. I believe that Zaccheus wanted to see the kind of man that would hang out with people like him. "I must see this one called Jesus because I have heard He hangs out with tax collectors. I heard that He goes to parties with tax collectors." Zaccheus was conflicted, because he had a desire to see Jesus, but on the other hand, he had a concern about being seen *by* Jesus. Zaccheus may have thought, "How can I see Jesus without Him seeing me? He is coming this way. I will climb up into a tree, where I can get a good view of Him, but at the same time I will limit how close He gets to me." Zaccheus knew that he was unworthy. He decided to climb up into a sycamore tree.

Hiding in the Sycamore Tree

A sycamore tree is a cross between a mulberry tree and a fig tree. It is the size of a mulberry tree, about eight feet in circumference, but it has the fruit of a fig tree. In that day, people would line the roads with sycamore trees for two reasons. One was to make the area more beautiful, and the other reason was to provide food for the people that were poor. If you couldn't afford to buy food, you could walk along the road and partake freely of the figs on the sycamore trees without cost. Here is Zaccheus, a very rich man, up a poor man's tree. God sure has a sense of humor! I can imagine this little man peering through the fig leaves wanting to see Jesus. "I must get a closer look at this man, but it's hard to hide behind the fig leaves and still see."

Adam tried hiding behind fig leaves after he and Eve had sinned. As soon as they realized they had failed God, they were afraid and became ashamed of their nakedness. In their shame, they covered themselves with fig leaves (Genesis 3:10) which were totally inadequate. It's no wonder the only tree on record that Jesus cursed during His earthly ministry was a fig tree. It represents the hiding place. It is where you hide when you don't want to be seen, when you are ashamed of yourself, when you feel unworthy and inadequate, when you feel like a failure. Adam said, "I was afraid when I saw I was naked, and I hid myself." Like Adam and Eve, Zaccheus also hid behind fig leaves.

This is a picture of human nature, which tends to run to fig leaves instead of running to Calvary. Zaccheus, in his fallenness, in his failure, in his weakness, thought the same thing that Adam thought and that every other person has thought: "If God sees me like I really am, He will not love me."

Is that not the reason we hide? We hide for fear that if the shame of our "nakedness" is apparent, we will not be loved. We say, "If they only knew what I was really like, they wouldn't love me." Have you ever thought that? We hide, but it's a deception of the enemy, because the love of God isn't like the love of men. When God came into the garden looking for Adam, He wasn't looking to condemn him. He was interested in restoring the closeness they once enjoyed.

Time to Come Out of Hiding

How often we hide. We hide behind our language. We know what to say and when to say it. We know what songs to sing and when to clap our hands in church. We hide behind our busyness. We hide behind our friends. We are always hiding. It appeared that Zaccheus was successful in his hiding, except that as Jesus got closer to that tree, He suddenly stopped. Picture a whole group of people following Jesus. When He stopped, they stopped. "Why is He stopping here?" Then they saw Him look up into that tree. "What is He looking at?" "I don't know.

It looks like a little kid up there." Jesus says, "Zaccheus!" Talk about being identified! Jesus could have said, "You up there," but instead He called Zaccheus by name. "Zaccheus, get down from there right now." I can imagine some of the very devout people saying, "Oh boy, he is going to 'get it' now! Payback time. That little guy deserves it. He ripped me off. Get him, Jesus." Jesus said, "Do you think you can hide from Me? I have been searching for you." In Genesis 3:9, God said, "Adam, where art thou?" Do you think for a minute that God didn't know where Adam was? He knew exactly where he was. He just wanted Adam to admit where he was.

Jesus was saying to Zaccheus, "The day of hiding is over. The day of shame is over. The day of walking around with your head down is over. I am coming by your tree today. You have been up in the tree too long." The next thing He said is one of the most powerful things that could ever be said. He said, "Zaccheus, I want to go abide at your house." I believe there are two reasons He said that. First of all, Jesus was saying, "I am going to get involved in your business. I am going to mess with your priorities. I am going to mess with what you are all about. I am going to mess with what you are doing. I am going to get involved in your life." Suppose that you met Jesus on the street today, and He said to you, "I am going home with you right now." Would you be nervous about what He might find in your home?

It's Personal

I believe that Jesus was saying to Zaccheus, "What is happening between you and I is very personal and very private. There are too many people standing around here that want to eavesdrop." I am so very glad that we serve a God like this. When He deals with us, it is very personal. He doesn't broadcast our issues over a loudspeaker to the public. It's between you and Jesus. In Psalm 51:4, David said, "Against Thee only, O God, have I sinned." God is interested in restoration and healing. He is not interested in destruction and ruin. You need to be very careful who you talk to and what you say, because not everyone that calls himself by Jesus' name is like Him. Jesus said, "Come on, Zaccheus. You and I need to talk." The two of them went together to Zaccheus' house, and the Word of God states that the people began to murmur. They were upset, irritated, and aggravated. "How could Jesus do that? That man is unclean. That man's house is unclean. Why is Jesus going with him to his house?" They didn't understand the unfeigned love of God. Even today, many people don't understand it. We only understand it to the extent it has been revealed. When God gives a little mercy and grace to us, and He blesses us and forgives us, we sometimes put on "religious robes" and we start judging everyone that we don't think is where we are spiritually.

Jesus could have read Zaccheus "the riot act" right there. "I am going to tell you what you have done. I am going to tell you who you stole from. I am going to embarrass you." Instead, He said, "Zaccheus, it's just Me and you." That really irritated the religious people.

A number of years ago, *Time* magazine profiled a telephone line where people could call in and confess what they did wrong. They were receiving two hundred calls a day because people could call in and feel some relief of guilt without judgment because nobody answered the phone. The calls were routed to an answering machine or voice mailbox. Then a second line was added, and there was a charge to call this second line. You could call in on that line and listen to the confessions of the people who had called the first line. On that second line, even though people had to pay, they were getting ten thousand calls a day. People tend to like to hear other people's "dirt." "Well, what did you hear about so and so? I can pray a lot more effectively if you give me the details." The religious people were irritated with Jesus and Zaccheus. They wanted to see Jesus condemn him and rebuke him. They thought that they were about to get even with Zaccheus, and instead, Jesus was going to his home. What an outrage!

When Jesus got into Zaccheus' house, something happened to Zaccheus. It doesn't say that Jesus identified all of Zaccheus' failures, or that Jesus opened his accounting books to expose his cheating ways. Instead, when the unfeigned love of God filled that house, Zaccheus wanted to do something he didn't want to do before. He wanted to be a giver. Romans 2:4 declares, "It is the goodness of God that leads us to repentance." God starts loving you so much, and it gets so heavy that you can't handle it. You are changed, and you are inspired to love and to give. Jesus didn't call him out of the tree with a judge's gavel. He called him out of the tree with a plan for salvation, which results in wholeness.

When Jesus came to Zaccheus' house, wholeness came to his house. Zaccheus suddenly spoke up and said, "Jesus, everyone that I have stolen from, everyone that I have wronged, I am going to give them back four times what I took." If a man was caught stealing from another, according to the law, he had to pay back what he took plus twenty percent. That is all the law required, but when the unfeigned love of God fills you, you go far beyond what is required. People that are living by law are missing something. Zaccheus said, "Even beyond returning what I have taken, I am going to take half of everything I have and give it to whoever has a need." Zaccheus was not looking for fig leaves to hide behind any more. He was looking for people that needed figs! What a miracle of grace and transformation. Zaccheus came out of his tree because Someone loved him into wholeness.

The Joy of Being Found

One of my little grandsons liked to play hide and seek. He always wanted to do the hiding, and he wanted me to do the seeking. He wasn't a good hider at all. Half of him was sticking out no matter where he hid, but I would play along with him. I would go around, and I would say, "Where is he? My, he is hiding so well." Finally I would say, "Where are you?" And he would say, "Here I am!" I used to think the little guy didn't understand the game because you are not supposed to tell where you are. One day, I felt that the Lord spoke to my heart, and said, "Do you know why he does that? Because he knows as soon as he says

'Here I am' that you are going to hug him, kiss him, and laugh together, and then he is going to say, 'Papa, let's do it again.'"

My grandson was willing to come out of hiding because he knew he was going to be loved when he got out. I believe he learned something that many people have never learned. He learned that the fun wasn't in the hiding; the fun was in coming out of hiding and getting loved. "Papa, do it again." It is fun being found and being loved. I believe Zaccheus would say the same thing. He would say, "Do you know when the fun started? When I came out from behind the fig leaves and came down from the tree! I thought I knew what life was all about. I was trying to find fulfillment and success, but I was miserable. Life really started for me when Jesus stopped under my tree and He said, 'Come on out from your hiding place.'"

God had no sooner found Adam and Eve than He gave them the promise of redemption in Genesis 3:15. He put His arms around their fallen-ness, their failure, and their darkness, and He said, "I want you to know something. There will come a Seed from a woman, and the Seed is going to bruise the head of the serpent. It will take a few years, but I want you to know that the game doesn't end with you coming out of hiding. That is just the beginning. That is when the fun starts. That is when it all makes sense."

Even today, Jesus looks up into our trees, seeing through the fig leaves. He comes with a kind of love that won't rip you up, tear you down, or throw you in the gutter. I am speaking of a love that will heal every hurt, bridge every chasm, restore your heart, and change your life forever. It's called the unfeigned love of God.

Chapter 4

Love That Sees, Cares, and Heals

John 9:1-16 states, "And as Jesus passed by, He saw a man which was blind from his birth. And His disciples asked Him saying, Master, who did sin, this man or his parents, that he was born blind? And Jesus answered, Neither hath this man sinned nor his parents but that the works of God should be made manifest in him. I must work the works of Him that sent Me while it is day. The night cometh when no man can work. As long as I am in the world, I am the light of the world. And when He had thus spoken, He spat on the ground and made clay of the spittle, and He anointed the eyes of the blind man with the clay. And He said unto him, Go wash in the pool of Siloam, (which is by interpretation, Sent). He went his way therefore and washed, and came seeing. The neighbors, therefore, and they which before had seen him that he was blind, said, Is not this he that sat and begged?" Some said, This is he. Others said, Well, he is like him. But he said, I am he. Therefore said they unto him, how were thine eyes opened? He answered and said, A man that is called Jesus made clay and anointed mine eyes, and He said unto me, Go to the pool of Siloam and wash, and I went and I washed and I received sight. Then said they unto him, Where is He? He said, I know not. They brought to the Pharisees him that aforetime was blind. And it was the Sabbath Day when Jesus made clay and opened his eyes. Then again the Pharisees also asked him how he had received his sight. He said unto them, He put clay upon mine eyes and I washed and do see. And therefore, said some of the Pharisees, This man is not of God because He keepeth not the Sabbath day. Others said, How can a man that is a sinner do such miracles? And there was a division among them.

Verse 18 states, "The Jews did not believe concerning him that he had been blind and received his sight until they called the parents of him that had received his sight." They asked the parents about the matter, and finally the parents said to them, "Look, we don't know who did this. We don't know when it happened, but we do know our son was born blind and now he sees. He is of age. Ask him. He can speak for himself."

Passing By

Please note that the passage starts out, "And as Jesus passed by." Another translation reads, "As Jesus walked along." In the earthly ministry of Jesus, touching the lives of the hurting, the wounded, the lost, the confused, and the dying took place on a regular daily basis in a very non-sensational way. Please note here and throughout the Gospels that most of the miracles that Jesus performed were not performed in the synagogue or in the temple. Many weren't performed before large crowds. Jesus walked in the power and anointing of the Holy Spirit such that these things happened as He went along, as He "passed by." I am looking for God to work through His church like that in an ever increasing manner. I am expecting to see the day that, while we are at work, while we are driving down the highway, while we are having lunch, or while we are at the coffee machine, the Spirit of the Lord will come upon us, and right then and there someone will get saved or healed, a life will be changed, a captive will be set free. We must understand that walking with Jesus is a lifestyle. It's not a program. It's not something that is limited to when we come together at a certain specified time to give and receive ministry. This must go beyond the walls of the churches. It must go beyond the synagogues and beyond the temples. God is interested in touching people right where they are. Miracles happened "as Jesus passed by."

The Neighbors' Reaction

"As Jesus passed by, He saw a man who was blind from birth."
John gives us a little more insight into this situation. Verses 8 and
9 say that after he had been healed, the neighbors couldn't even
agree whether this was the same man who had been blind and
begging. Isn't that interesting? He had been blind from birth.
He had undoubtedly been there in their midst for twenty, thirty,
or more years. They passed by him frequently, but they had so
completely ignored him that they weren't even sure he was the
same man that had been blind. Even his neighbors couldn't
even identify him after God had touched his eyes. This man had
lived a life of anonymity. It was as if he had been invisible. He
was there, yet nobody saw him. He was sitting there blind and
begging, but most people walked right on by. Most people didn't
take the time or effort to even stop and consider his situation.
Over the years, he grew accustomed to being ignored. By their
actions, people were saying he was not even worth noticing.
Many people were repulsed by him for several reasons. As a
blind man, to pay attention to him was depressing. As a beggar,
to pay attention to him was demanding. As a product of sin,
which many of them considered him to be, to pay attention to
him was disgusting. Mothers took their children by the hand
as they passed by this depressing, demanding, and disgusting
man and said, "Don't look that way or listen to that man. Just
pretend like you don't see him and keep on walking. Ignore
him." The man was there, yet not there. He was not a part of
the happenings. He was ignored.

The Pain of Being Ignored

There are probably few kinds of pain in the world that can
compare to the pain of being ignored. A husband and wife sit
at the table. He is reading the newspaper. She is pouring out
her heart to him. After a while she gets very frustrated and
says to him, "You are not listening to me." He replies, "Oh, yes
I am. I can repeat every word you said." And he proceeds to
demonstrate by repeating almost word for word everything
that she has said. But is she satisfied? No, because she could

buy a tape recorder to do that. She says, "I want you to be fully emotionally present. I want you to put down the newspaper. I want you to look me in the eyes." She says, in effect, "I don't want simply to be listened to. I want to be attended to. I don't want to be ignored."

We are that way when we are brought into the world. Babies, we are told, have three requirements in life. One is food, another is water, and a third is attention. Attention is one of the most powerful forces in the entire world. Babies need a human face to look at. They lie in their crib and smile, and the human face smiles back. Psychologists call that *attunement*, which is connecting with another human being, tuning in to someone else, and being on the same wavelength. Even though a baby cannot express himself in words, he is watching the face. He knows that whatever he is doing is getting a response from the face. He's being attended to. The baby is saying, "I know I matter to someone. I know someone cares." When that face disappears, many times the baby cries because he needs the attention. That face is like a mirror to that little baby. He knows when he is doing something good, and he knows when he is doing something wrong. Attunement is important to human beings.

Our Need for Attention

Some time ago, I read about an experiment that was conducted at a college. I share this to illustrate that as we grow and mature, we continue to have the same need for attunement. In this particular experiment, all of the members of a class were instructed to respond to someone that would give a signal while the professor was lecturing. They started the experiment by slouching down in their chairs with no eye contact, staring at the ceiling. The professor was giving the lesson in somewhat of a monotone manner, mumbling through his notes. Then a signal was given to all of the students, and suddenly they all sat up on the edge of their seats, and they began to look at, and focus on, the professor. The professor began to change how he talked. He began to talk faster and more energetically, using gestures to emphasize his words. The students received another signal, and they all went back to slouching. Painfully, he slipped back into the monotone, mumbling through his notes. The professor was responding to the attention, the attunement.

Sometimes when I am preaching, I will stop for a moment and "read" the audience. It helps me to see whether I am being clear, whether I have made my point, and whether I can proceed. An audience provides help and feedback to a speaker through their attention and attunement. One of the most marvelous miracles in the world is that God pays attention to us.

In Numbers 6:24-26, The Lord effectively said to Moses, "Go tell Aaron and his sons to go before the children of Israel, because I want you to bless them. You are to say 'The Lord bless you and keep you. The Lord make His face to shine upon you and be gracious unto you. The Lord lift up His countenance upon you and give you peace.'" What was God saying that He wanted the children of Israel to know? "The Lord make His countenance to shine upon you." Another translation is clearer when it says, "The Lord turn His face toward you." (NIV) God was saying, "I want you to tell My people that I turn My face toward them. I want My people to know that I really care about them." When you turn your face to someone, you are fully devoted to them. He said, "I want My people to know that I don't desire to be doing other things. I enjoy focusing on you." Lord, help us to understand this truth! Our problem is that we look in the mirror and we can't figure out why God would say, "You are more important to Me than anything else. I have my eye on you. I am fully devoted to you." The other part of that verse is "to make His face shine upon you." That means He shows delight when He looks at you, like when a parent looks at their baby and smiles. He says, "I find delight in looking at you." That kind of expression occurs when we love someone very deeply.

I believe David understood this. In Psalm 27:8-9 he said, "God, Thou saidst to me turn, turn your face toward Me. Set your face upon Me. Seek My face. When you said, Lord, seek My face, my heart said unto You, Thy face will I seek." Today, many people are only seeking His *hand*. They are saying, "Give me, give me, give me." There is something better, and that is seeking His *face*. David cried out to God as if in pain, "God, don't hide Your face far from me. I need Your face. I can't make it without Your face. I must have Your face, Your delight, Your attention." It is an interesting play on words that attention is so valuable that we don't "give attention." We "pay attention." You *pay* attention. It *costs* you something to pay attention to someone else.

The Disciples' Reaction

Because Jesus saw this man who was blind from birth, the disciples noticed him. However, when the disciples saw the man, they didn't see him like Jesus saw him. When they saw him, he became a theological discussion. Chronologically, right before this, Jesus had sent the disciples out to minister (Luke 10:1-17). They had healed the sick and cast out devils, and they came back rejoicing that demons were subject unto His name. After that glorious ministry, they saw this blind man, but instead of ministering to him, they entered into a discussion. "Peter, who do you think sinned? I'll bet it was his parents." "No, I don't think it was his parents. I think it was him." "What do you think, Thomas? Was it he or his parents that sinned?" They couldn't agree on the matter, so they went to Jesus and they said, "Jesus, we would like to know who sinned that caused this man's blindness. It is important to us, Jesus. We know he needs to be healed, but let's deal with the cause of this first. Who sinned, Jesus? Was it the man or his parents?"

If you didn't know anything about the traditions and customs of that time, you might think that this was a dumb question. How could it be his fault if he was born blind? In that time, they believed that it was possible for a fetus to sin. If a mother, while carrying a child, sinned by going into an idolatrous temple, for example, they believed that the sin was passed along to the child. The disciples were consumed with the cause of this man's blindness. They saw an interesting theological question, rather than a blind, hurting, discouraged, ignored, disappointed, and rejected man. Unfortunately, there are still these kinds of disciples around today. "Oh, you are sick? There must be sin in your life."

They believed in cause-and-effect. If they saw the effect of someone blind, they knew there had to be a cause. "What is the cause? Who caused it? There must be sin in the camp." I want to say to these disciples, "Get out of the way and let Jesus heal this man!"

Romans 14:10 states, "Why doest thou judge thy brother and why doest thou set at naught thy brother?" The phrase "set at naught" means "to look down on" in the Greek language. We must not look down on people. Instead, we need to lift them up, encourage them, strengthen them, bless them, feed them, and do everything we can for them. The last phrase of Romans 14:10 states, "Because we are all going to stand before the judgment seat of Christ." The disciples only saw the man because Jesus had seen him first, and then they got sidetracked by theology. Jesus said, "You that said it was his parents that sinned, you are wrong." I can just hear the other group saying, "We knew we were right. It was the man that sinned!" Then Jesus turned to them and He said, "You are wrong, too." It is pretty deflating when you are a disciple and your theology is wrong! I learned many years ago that there is an awful lot I don't know. But there is *Someone* I do know, and I want to listen to what *He* says. I want to get out of His way and let Him do His wondrous works.

Jesus moved the bickering disciples out of the way and went to the blind man. Jesus spit on the ground, mixed the spittle with a little dust, took the clay, and put it on the man's eyes. He said, "Go down and wash at the pool of Siloam, and you will be healed." I can't prove this from Scripture, but I believe Jesus performed a creative miracle. In the beginning, God reached into the dust of the earth when He made the first man. Thousands of years later, I believe that Jesus reached into the dust of earth to make new eyeballs for this man. Jesus saw him in his place of need. To Jesus, he was not a man to be ignored, nor an object of theological debate. To Jesus, he was a hurting, wounded, and abandoned man that needed wholeness. Jesus didn't just *see* him. He also *cared* about him.

There is an old hymn that declares, "No one ever cared for me like Jesus. There's no other friend so kind as He. No one else could take the sin and darkness from me. Oh how much He cares for me." We are speaking of the kind of love that _sees_, _cares_, and _heals_. This love *sees* our need. This love *cares* so much that it can't stop with seeing and caring; it must *heal*. Jesus couldn't stop with seeing and caring. He had to heal, because this kind of love is not satisfied until it heals. This man had become the object of the attention of the Master even though the neighbors had ignored him. Who cares what the neighbors think anyway? It's what *Jesus* thinks and does that really matters.

The Parents' Reaction

People-pleasing only gets us in trouble. That was the case with the blind man's parents. They didn't do a good job of defending him. They kept saying, "We don't know. Ask him." John gives us some insight into the parents' reaction. He wrote that the reason they acted like that was because they were afraid they would get thrown out of the synagogue. Religion is too often about pleasing, satisfying, and honoring people, rather than God.

The Pharisees' Reaction

The Pharisees said, "We must get to the bottom of this. The issue was not _whether_ he was healed, but rather _when_ he was healed. According to our understanding, this can't be tolerated on a Sabbath day." If we are going to walk with Jesus, we need to burn our religious calendar, because Jesus doesn't operate on our timetable. The Pharisees were upset because this healing was a threat to their religion and everything they were about.

The Pharisees had thirty-nine major things that were forbidden on the Sabbath, and many of them had subcategories. For example, you couldn't pull a hair out of your head or cut your fingernails on the Sabbath Day. You couldn't make clay or knead dough. I was startled to discover that one of the other things that wasn't permitted on the Sabbath was making someone better. If someone was dying, you could do whatever you needed to do to keep them alive, but you couldn't do anything to make them better. If someone sprained an ankle, you could not pour cold water on it, because it might help to heal it. Jesus was violating their man-made rules. He not only healed a man, but He made clay to do it.

Have you ever had to unlearn something that you thought was absolutely true? You were so sure of it that you would argue with your last breath. You were absolutely, positively, unquestionably, unconditionally sure. That mentality can cause us trouble. We are continuously learning. The one constant is Jesus. We don't need anything but Him, just Him. How could the Pharisees get so far off track that the most important thing to them was not the healing of a person but rather when it occurred? The Pharisees didn't *see* this man like Jesus saw him, and that is why they couldn't *do* for this man what Jesus could do for him. The disciples didn't *see*, and they couldn't *do*. The parents didn't *see*, and they couldn't *do*. The neighbors didn't *see*, and they couldn't *do* either.

Here Comes Jesus

But here comes the unfeigned love of God, the kind of love that doesn't care about who sinned or who didn't sin, that doesn't care about what day of the week it is, that isn't ashamed to stand up and confess truth, and that will not ignore or turn away from even those who not appealing nor pleasant. Here comes the unfeigned love of God. Here comes Jesus.

Perhaps you can identify in some way with this blind man. Perhaps you have been ignored, like the neighbors ignored him. Perhaps you have been misjudged, like the disciples misjudged him. Perhaps you have been accused, like the Pharisees accused him. Perhaps you have been abandoned, like his parents abandoned him. Perhaps you have been sitting by the side of the road needing attention, needing a touch, needing someone to care about you. Perhaps you need someone to see where you are and to feel what you feel. Someone that has the power to change everything and make things as they should be, to make you whole. The good news is that He is passing your way. His name is Jesus. He is passing by. His is the kind of love that sees, cares, and heals. He wants to make you whole.

Chapter 5

He's Sitting On Your Well

John 4:1-30 states, "Therefore when the Lord knew how the Pharisees had heard that Jesus made and baptized more disciples than John (though Jesus Himself baptized not but His disciples), He left Judea and departed again into Galilee. And He must needs go through Samaria. Then cometh He to a city of Samaria which is called Sychar, near to the parcel of ground that Jacob gave to his son Joseph. Now Jacob's well was there. Jesus therefore, being wearied with His journey, sat thus on the well. And it was about the sixth hour. There cometh a woman of Samaria to draw water: Jesus saith unto her, Give Me to drink. (For His disciples were gone away unto the city to buy meat.) Then saith the woman of Samaria unto him, How is it that thou, being a Jew, askest drink of me, which am a woman of Samaria? For the Jews have no dealings with the Samaritans. Jesus answered and said unto her, If thou knewest the gift of God, and who it is that saith to thee, Give me to drink; thou wouldest have asked of him, and he would have given thee living water. "

"The woman saith unto him, Sir, thou hast nothing to draw with, and the well is deep: from whence then hast thou that living water? Art thou greater than our father Jacob, which gave us the well, and drank thereof himself, and his children, and his cattle? Jesus answered and said unto her, Whosoever drinketh of this water shall thirst again: But whosoever drinketh of the water that I shall give him shall never thirst; but the water that I shall give him shall be in him a well of water springing up into everlasting life. The woman saith unto him, Sir, give me this water, that I thirst not, neither come hither to draw. Jesus saith unto her, Go, call thy husband, and come hither. The woman answered and said, I have no husband. Jesus said unto her, Thou hast well said, I have no husband: For thou hast had five husbands; and he whom thou now hast is not thy husband: in that saidst thou truly."

"The woman saith unto him, Sir, I perceive that thou art a prophet. Our fathers worshipped in this mountain; and ye say, that in Jerusalem is the place where men ought to worship. Jesus saith unto her, Woman, believe me, the hour cometh, when ye shall neither in this mountain, nor yet at Jerusalem, worship the Father. Ye worship ye know not what: we know what we worship: for salvation is of the Jews. But the hour cometh, and now is, when the true worshippers shall worship the Father in spirit and in truth: for the Father seeketh such to worship him. God is a Spirit: and they that worship him must worship him in spirit and in truth. The woman saith unto him, I know that Messias cometh, which is called Christ: when he is come, he will tell us all things. Jesus saith unto her, I that speak unto thee am he. And upon this came his disciples, and marveled that he talked with the woman: yet no man said, What seekest thou? Or, Why talkest thou with her? The woman then left her water pot, and went her way into the city, and saith to the men, Come, see a man, which told me all things that ever I did: is not this the Christ? Then they went out of the city, and came unto him."

A Divine Appointment at the Well

At that time in history, Israel was divided into three major territories. To the north was Galilee, the central area was Samaria, and to the south was Judea. There was great animosity between the people of Samaria and the Jews that were in both Galilee and Judea. In fact, it was common for Jews to avoid even passing through Samaria while traveling. Jews that were traveling from Judea north to Galilee, as Jesus was about to do, or south from Galilee to Judea, would cross the Jordan river to the east, travel through the land of Perea, and then cross the

Jordan again back into Israel. The Jews in Judea and Galilee considered themselves somewhat superior to the Samaritans and therefore looked down upon them. In most cases, the Jews wanted nothing to do with the Samaritans. John 4:9 states, "They have no dealings with them."

I am thankful that Jesus isn't like that. He doesn't look down on people, and He doesn't circumvent or avoid things that need dealt with. He confronts what needs to be confronted, directly, firmly, and lovingly, and He does it to the glory of God and the betterment of each of us, His children. John's Gospel tells us that Jesus was *compelled* to go through Samaria. Jesus was led by the Father, by the Spirit of the Lord, to take the unpopular route through Samaria. Jesus said that He only did what He saw the Father do (John 5:19), so I believe that it was His Father's perfect will that Jesus take this particular route at this particular time. Jesus had a divine appointment with a woman at a well.

John 4:8 tells us that Jesus' disciples went to get some lunch. It was around noontime, and Jesus was left alone at the well. This particular well that Jesus chose to visit by divine direction was known as Jacob's well, and it had great historical significance.

Samaritans, Sychar, and Shechem

The Samaritans were an Israelite sect that had their sanctuary on Mount Gerizim, near the city of Shechem. They believed that Joshua had built a sanctuary there years before, and they traced themselves back to Jacob. In Genesis 12:6-7, God said to Abraham, "Unto thy seed will I give this land." Abraham was in the land of Shechem when God gave that specific promise to him. Jacob was the son of Isaac, who was the son of Abraham. Jacob had moved into this land, bought a parcel for a burial ground, and built an altar. Jacob also dug a well in Shechem, and this is the very well, *Jacob's well*, where this event in John 4:1-30 transpired.

Jesus came to this well near the city of Sychar (John 4:5), and theologians and historians believe that Sychar and Shechem are the exact same place. Jesus was at the exact spot which God had promised to Abraham's seed, where Jacob dug a well, made an altar, and purchased a burial ground. Way back in Genesis, God said, "This is the place I am going to meet with My people in a special way." This well called Jacob's well is very significant, and Scripture takes great care to mention it. The Bible doesn't state that Jesus stopped at *a* well or *the* well. It declares that He stopped at *Jacob's* well. When Scripture mentions a person, place, or thing by name, it means that the Holy Spirit wants to bring something important to our attention, and in this instance, it means that in order to understand what God wants to communicate to us through this story, we must learn more about Jacob's well and the man for which it was named.

Jacob's Well

Jacob was considered to be a man of conflicting natures. He was a "man of mixture." He had two opposing natures in him. If you study Jacob's life, you will identify certain things about him. He cheated and he lied. He was crafty, cunning, deceitful, and full of guile. He was mean, prideful, and selfish. He was unprincipled in many areas of his life. But he also had another side, another "nature" in him. At times he was affectionate, loving, and prayerful. There were times that he demonstrated great faith, and times that he was very industrious. There were some very positive things about Jacob, and some very negative things about Jacob as well. These two conflicting natures existed in this one man. People never knew which of Jacob's two natures was going to manifest in any given situation. They never knew what to expect of him. They never knew how he was going to respond because of these two diverse natures that existed in him. He was a man of mixture.

Abraham, Isaac, and Jacob are the patriarchs of our faith. We say of Abraham, "There is a man of faith. He believed God and it was accounted unto him for righteousness." We look at Isaac and say, "There is a man of obedience, who submitted himself to the altar as a sacrifice before God." What about Jacob, the man with the "dual nature?"

We, as born again believers, can identify with Jacob, because we all have this dual nature within us. In Romans 8 and Galatians 5, the Apostle Paul writes that this dual nature exists in New Covenant believers. He said there is an internal conflict between two warring factions inside of us, called our _flesh_ and our _spirit_. Termed _regeneration_, our human spirit comes alive when we are born again. We all wish that when the spirit nature comes alive, the flesh nature would die, but it doesn't. In fact, Galatians 5:16 tells us that it's only as we walk in the Spirit that the lusts of the flesh are not fulfilled. It doesn't say that the lusts of the flesh are "not experienced," but rather "not fulfilled." Galatians 5:17 declares that the flesh nature wars against the Spirit nature, and the Spirit nature wars against the flesh nature, so there is contention in our inner being. Jacob was not only a man, but he is very much an example, a symbol, a type, with which we can identify. We all have a flesh nature that wrestles for our attention and wants to have its own way. In the Bible, the Apostle Paul wrote about some characteristics of the flesh nature, which we often call the 'old man.' In Galatians 5:19, Paul wrote, "The works of the flesh are manifest which are these..." The word "works" means "inclinations, desires, and the things that the flesh wants to do, and will do, if unchecked."

Paul identifies the works of the flesh in Galatians 5:19-21, "Adultery, fornication, uncleanness, lasciviousness," which means indecency, "idolatry, witchcraft, hatred, variances, contentions," quarreling, "seditions, wrath, strife, heresies, envyings, murders, drunkenness, revellings." We must recognize the potential in each of us to yield to the works of the flesh. It has always been of interest to me that at the Last Supper when Jesus said, "One of you is going to betray Me," every one of the disciples said, "Is it I?" It is apparent that the disciples recognized the potential in themselves to do the wrong thing, to follow the flesh rather than the spirit.

Galatians 5:22 speaks of the other nature, the character of God when it declares, "But the fruit of the Spirit is love, joy, peace, long-suffering, kindness, gentleness, meekness, temperance, faith. Against such there is no law." There is a nature in us that desires to express itself through the fruit of the Spirit, and there is also a nature in us that desires to express itself through the works of the flesh. Don't let the devil tell you that you are not a Christian when you feel something you shouldn't feel, think something you shouldn't think, or do something you shouldn't do. He is a liar.

The Devil Made Me Do It?

I believe that sometimes we blame things on demons that should be blamed on the flesh. It is true that people sometimes have demonic oppression or strongholds in their lives, but not every little wrong feeling or thought that we experience is demonically influenced. We blame demons rather than accept any personal responsibility for it. We tend to want to blame everyone else. Comedian Flip Wilson used to say, "The devil made me do it." It was funny, but not accurate. If you are a Christian, the devil can't make you do anything. The devil simply presents an opportunity for you to do it. Scripture declares, "Walk in the Spirit and you won't fulfill the lusts of the flesh." We must learn how to walk in the Spirit. God is working in our lives to make us into everything He wants us to be. Occasionally you may notice something in you that you thought and hoped was no longer there, and the devil will jump on your shoulder and say, "See, you are no good. You will never be any good. I told you that. Do you believe me now?" But what is really happening? God has just unveiled something that He is going to deal with in your life.

Jesus was going through Samaria, and He made a point to go to Sychar to Jacob's well. When He arrived at Jacob's well, He sat on it. That wasn't accidental. Jesus chose *Jacob's well*, and He purposely chose to sit on it. Jacob's well represents the flesh nature in each of our lives, and our internal struggle between the flesh nature and the spirit nature.

What's He Doing on the Well?

Around noon, a woman came with her water pot to draw water from Jacob's well, as she did every day. However, this day was unlike any other day, because Jesus was sitting on the well.

"Pardon me Sir. Kindly move over and get out of the way, because I have something to do. Sir, you are hindering me." Jesus was sitting on the well effectively saying by His very presence there, "If you are going to draw water out of this well, you are going to have to get by Me." This may have frustrated the woman. She had never known anything her whole life except drawing water from Jacob's well. That is all she ever had to quench her thirst, but her deepest thirst had never been quenched. Not only was she living out of Jacob's well in a literal sense, but also in a spiritual sense. She had been living out of the flesh nature all her whole life. She already had five husbands and she was living with a sixth man, and it's as if Jesus was sitting there and saying "Okay, your days of living out of Jacob's well are over. If you are going to get water out of this well, you are going to have to get by Me to do it."

The woman must have wondered, "What is this all about? What is He doing sitting there? He has never been there before." Jesus said to her, "I want you to give Me a drink." Did Jesus really want water out of Jacob's well? No, He was going to start revealing something to that woman that would turn her whole life around. She was never going to have to live the same way that she had lived before. Perhaps the woman was thinking, "I don't know why He wants to talk to me. If He knew about me, my past, and my failings, He wouldn't be spending time with me." But the problem was not that He didn't know *her*; the problem was that she did not know *Him*.

I believe what Jesus saw in her is not what she _was_ but what she _could be_. He saw her potential. He saw that she had the potential of turning a whole city around. This ordinary sin-stained woman with a water pot had the potential of setting a whole city on fire for God! He said, "Give Me a drink." She said, "But You are a Jew and I am a Samaritan. Why are you here, and why are you asking me for anything?"

Isn't it glorious that Jesus reached down in the middle of the millions of people in this world and touched our lives? Think about that for a minute. It's overwhelming. One day He walked through the darkness, the brokenness, the weakness, and the failures of our lives, He confronted us, and He said, "You have something I want." Jesus came and "sat on the well" of our lives to get our attention.

This woman couldn't put it all together in her mind. Neither can we. Like the woman, you may think, "Lord, why did You come to me? If You knew everything I have ever done and thought..." He *does* know what you have done and thought. Not only that, but He also knows what you are going to do and think in the future, and yet He still confronts you by "sitting on your well." When you fail, don't be dismayed, because He knew you were going to fail before He sat on your well. This entire dialogue between Jesus and the woman takes place with Him sitting on her well. Jesus didn't get off her well. Once He gets on your well, He will not get off. He loves us too much to get off of our wells. When He is there, we see our own sinfulness and His goodness, and we are convicted by the Holy Spirit that there is something better than the water from the well on which we've been living.

Bucket Believer

Jesus said, "I am sitting on your well, and I am going to sit here until you allow Me to change some things in your life for the better." She said, "But you are a Jew, and I am a Samaritan, and I thought Jews looked down on Samaritans." She was now beginning to understand that her concept of Him was all wrong. He was already beginning to change her thinking. He said to her, "If you knew who I am, you would ask Me for water."

Isn't it beautiful the way Jesus teaches us line upon line, precept upon precept, little by little? He does that because we can't handle it all at once. This was an important dialogue going on between Jesus and the woman. They were going back and forth. He gave her a little bit of truth, He let her digest it, and then He gave her a little bit more truth. Then He repeated the process. He said, "The kind of water I am speaking of doesn't come out of Jacob's well. I am speaking of something that comes out of your innermost being. It's like a fountain. It flows out of you, and it not only nourishes you but it nourishes everyone that drinks of it. You have been a 'bucket believer.' You thought that the only way to live was bringing your bucket to Jacob's well every day and trying to handle the problems of the day out of Jacob's well." We are sometimes "bucket believers," trying to handle all of our thirst, situations, and circumstances out of Jacob's well. We try to make everything work from the water that we get out of Jacob's well. That is frustrating and unproductive. Jesus said, "The reason that I am here is to show you that there is something better."

Before we came to Jesus, we didn't know any better. The world is frustrated and confused because they are trying to draw from a well that doesn't satisfy. They think, "Perhaps if I get involved in this, or do this or do that, then I'll be fulfilled." They pull bucket after bucket out of the well, and Jesus is sitting there all of the time saying, "It doesn't matter how many buckets you draw out of that well. That water is not going to satisfy you. I have come to put a fountain in you because I know that what I created you to be can only come to pass if you have the fountain in you."

Did the woman ever change Samaria or Sychar when she was living by the water from Jacob's well? Never. She couldn't, because she didn't have the power. Jesus began to unfold the truth to her, and she began to understand His love. She began to understand that even though she didn't deserve it, earn it, or understand why He would do it, He had picked her out. He said to her, "I am going to show you a new way of living. The world teaches you that your happiness, joy, fulfillment, and satisfaction can be found in the well of the old nature. I am going to teach you where it's really found, and I am going to sit here on your well until you are ready to understand and receive it."

She kept trying to skirt the issue by changing the subject. She said, "Let's speak of worship for a while," and Jesus proceeded to share with her some important truths about worship, but the woman couldn't avoid what Jesus was ultimately there to do. She tried twice and couldn't do it. Likewise, you may try to ignore or avoid the deepest darkest issues in your life, but Jesus loves you too much to let you ignore them any longer. You keep trying, but you can't do it. He will sit on your well until you listen. The disciples were elsewhere getting lunch, but Jesus stayed at the well and He had unlimited time to give to the woman. He is just as patient in dealing with us. There has never been a well He couldn't sit on.

This dialogue continued until the woman finally understood. She had a breakthrough, a revelation. She said, "Jesus, give me this water You are speaking of, because I don't want to keep coming to this old well any more. I am tired of it. I don't want to live the rest of my life coming to this well. I don't want to live out of the flesh nature any longer. I want the water of which You speak." It took a while, but Jesus got through. He always does.

Repentance and Reception

She said, "Give me a drink. I am ready." Jesus said, "Before I give you water, we must deal with some things in your life. This is called 'repentance.'" I have a problem theologically with an "easy believe-ism" which simply says that all you have to do is believe in your heart and confess Jesus is Lord. The Bible declares that you must _repent_ for being a sinner. I don't mean you have to name every sin, but you have to say, "Lord, I have sinned and come short of Your glory." That is an important part of it.

Jesus said, "Go call your husband." Jesus was very wise. He didn't come to her and say, "You are a bad person. I know you have been married five times, and now you are living with a man that isn't your husband." Instead of rebuking her, He said, "Go call your husband." She probably thought, "Can we change the subject? Can we speak of worship again?" Have you ever tried to worship your way around repentance? Worship is so vitally important in our walk with Jesus, but it cannot take the place of repentance. Neither can good works.

The woman confessed. "Okay, Jesus, I will tell You. I don't have a husband." He said, "You are right. You don't. But you have had five of them and you are living with a sixth man now, who is not your husband." She was shocked and said, "Are You a prophet? I have never met a man like You before." Over the years, the woman had six men in her life, but none of them had met her deepest need. Jesus was the seventh man. The number seven in Scripture signifies completion. Jesus was the man that could truly complete her and fulfill her, where the other six could not.

She submitted herself to Jesus, and she got a drink. She received the fountain. She confessed that what He said about her was true. This was a personal thing between her and Jesus. Some people say you must publicly confess your sins to everyone. I don't believe that's scriptural. Jesus said very clearly, "This is between Me and you."

Leaving the Water Pot Behind

Please notice verse 28. The first thing she did was leave her water pot. Do you know why? She was never going to need it any more. She didn't just drop it and break it. She left it. That word means that she discarded it, effectively saying, "I don't need it." She was learning that the living water was not outside. It was inside. She left her water pot, ran into the city, and said to the men there, "Come see a man that told me everything I ever did." The part of this story that really thrills me is in verse 30, which tells us that when they heard her testimony "they went out of the city and came unto Him." They didn't run to her, they ran to Jesus. This was the first time in her life that she wasn't drawing men to her. She was drawing them to Him, because the well within lifts up Jesus.

The well within will cause people to want more of Him. People need to see Him, hear Him, thirst for Him, and want Him. The men came running to the well, and Jesus was sitting there on it. He said, "Do you want some living water too?" The city had been stirred because Jesus had refused to get off that well. He saw the potential in the woman, and He stayed there on the well until it was realized, until she came to a new level of living, ministry, and anointing. He stayed there until her life was changed. Jacob's well is still the same. If we are determined to draw water out of Jacob's well, we must circumvent Jesus because He will not move.

The disciples didn't understand everything that was going on. They came back and they saw Jesus talking to her, and they couldn't understand why He wasn't hungry. He said, "I have meat to eat that you don't know of." They may have thought someone else had brought Him lunch, but Jesus was speaking of the fulfillment and joy that He "filled up on" as He watched this woman's life be transformed by the living water.

Jesus touched a city because of one woman that was willing to leave her water pot at Jacob's well and say, "I am not going to live out of that well any longer." He is not going to give up on any of us either. Have you failed Him? He will not give up on you. He has created you and ordained you for a purpose. He has already determined what He is going to do with your life and with mine. When I see Him sitting on my well, I suddenly realize it's His mercy and His unfeigned love that keeps Him there. I don't deserve it and I can't earn it. I feel many times like He should abandon me, but I am so glad that He never will. Some of you may have heard the devil whisper in your ear, "God is done with you. He is through with you." That is a lie from the pit of hell, because what God starts, He finishes. What He begins, He completes. He is not only the Alpha, but He is the Omega. He is not only the First, but He is the Last. When you feel the discomfort, frustration, and weight of Him on your well, don't try to push Him off or go around Him. Simply lay down your bucket and say, "Give me that water, Lord. Make whatever changes You need to make in my life."

God's incredible, unfathomable, unfeigned love cannot be dampened by our failures, weaknesses or disappointments. He is committed to us to the very end. Jesus loves you. Don't try to figure out why. Just receive it. Accept it. Open your arms and say, "Lord, I am here and I am Yours."

Chapter 6

Inner Circle

The Apostle Paul wrote in II Corinthians 6:1-6, "We then, as workers together with Him, beseech you also that you receive not the grace of God in vain." In other words, there is a purpose, a divine design, for the grace of God coming to us. Parenthetically Paul wrote, "For He saith, I have heard thee in a time accepted, and in the day of salvation have I succored thee. Now is the accepted time, behold, now is the day of salvation. I don't want you to give offense in anything that the ministry be not blamed. But in all things approving ourselves as ministers of God in much patience, in afflictions, in necessities, in distresses, in stripes, in imprisonments, in tumults, in labors, in watchings, in fastings. By pureness, by knowledge, by long suffering, by kindness, by the Holy Ghost, by love unfeigned."

Peter, one of Jesus' inner circle, wrote in I Peter 1:22, "Seeing ye have purified your souls in obeying the truth through the Spirit unto unfeigned love of the brethren, see that ye love one another with a pure heart fervently."

God's Love Coming Through Us

In the first five chapters of this book, we have looked at the unfeigned love of God *to* us. Again, the word "unfeigned" means "genuine, real, pure, not pretentious, and not hypocritical." Beginning with this chapter, I want to take the next step and look at the unfeigned love of God *through* us. His love comes *to* us so that it might flow *through* us. Peter spoke of the "unfeigned love toward the brethren" and Paul reminds us that regardless of the situation—tumults, difficulties, or afflictions—the unfeigned love of God is manifest by the Holy Spirit.

During His earthly ministry, Jesus constantly demonstrated the unfeigned love of God. It didn't matter what the situation was before Him. It didn't matter how severe the need, nor whether the needy individual was a castoff or was highly respected. Jesus touched people right where they were with His love. His unfeigned love opened blind eyes, unstopped deaf ears, made the lame to walk, healed the sick, raised the dead, loved the children, received the publican, and forgave the prostitute.

Chosen to Follow Jesus

One day, after praying all night and receiving divine direction from His Father, Jesus chose twelve men to follow Him. They were not called simply to observe what He was doing, but rather to be so changed and transformed that when it came time for Him to return to His Father, they would continue with that same expression of unfeigned love. It was to flow through them, just as powerfully as He had demonstrated it, because it was the Father's purpose for His plan to continue from generation to generation. The kingdom that Jesus introduced will continue to expand until that glorious day when it literally swallows up all of the kingdoms of the world and He shall reign forevermore (Revelation 11:15).

A heavy calling was placed upon these twelve men, yet not unto them alone, but also unto us today. When the Holy Ghost came, He came to anoint the church, to empower the people of God to continue forward, and Jesus said, "Greater things than these that I do shall you do because I go to the Father."

Jesus didn't look at these men as though they were weak and incapable and say, "Do your best, and I hope you make it." No. Paul wrote in II Thessalonians 2:13, "God hath from the very beginning chosen you to salvation." God has chosen you. When that really gets into your spirit, it will change you. There is something God has done in your heart such that you can't be fully content doing anything else but loving Jesus and wanting to follow and obey Him, because He has chosen you. The devil sits on our shoulder and continually reminds us that God shouldn't have chosen us, that He made a mistake. The devil is a liar and the Word of God is forever true. God has chosen you.

Higher in Worship, Deeper in Prayer

I have spent time studying the lives of the twelve apostles that God chose. I preached a series of messages and wrote a book on the subject called *Chosen to Follow Jesus*. In those studies, I looked at their lives to learn what God had seen in them that He intended to use for His glory. Of the twelve that He chose, there were three—Peter, James, and John—whom we refer to as the "inner circle," that on occasion seemed to be closer to Jesus than the others. *They went higher in worship.* They were on the Mount of Transfiguration where Jesus was glorified and Moses and Elijah appeared. *They went deeper in prayer.* They went further into the Garden of Gethsemane as Jesus fought the battle of the ages for your soul and mine. They were also the only three that witnessed the overwhelming power of God as Jesus raised Jairus' daughter from the dead. We call these three men the "inner circle." Did Jesus love them more than the others? No, because Acts 10:34 states that God is "no respecter of persons." But there was a desire in their heart to draw closer to Jesus and be a part of everything He was doing. They didn't hesitate to climb the mountain, go into the garden at night, or enter Jairus' house where death reigned, as long as Jesus was there.

What seemed to set these three apart from the others? The book of Acts declares that they continued to manifest the unfeigned love of God. On the day of Pentecost, Peter stood up and preached a sermon and three thousand people were saved (Acts 2:14-41). Peter and John went to the temple and spoke the word "such as I *have* give I unto thee, in the name of Jesus" and the lame man stood and walked and leapt and praised God (Acts 3:1-11). Acts 4:18 tells us that the very lives of Peter and John were threatened for teaching in the name of Jesus, but they looked to their heavenly Father for a new boldness and anointing, and five thousand people were saved.

They, along with other believers, gathered together for a prayer meeting according to Acts 4:23-31, and the power of God fell, they were filled with the Holy Ghost, and mighty signs and wonders began to happen. These men had been transformed by the love and power of God.

What made Peter, James, and John unique? Apparently it wasn't their appearance, because the Bible doesn't mention that. Apparently it wasn't their education, because Acts 4:13 refers to them as "unlearned and ignorant men." Apparently it wasn't their outstanding personalities. These men wouldn't qualify as dynamic leaders according to the leadership books written today.

Provision, Protection, Promotion

They weren't there because they were good *providers*. Jesus, a carpenter, had to tell them how to fish! "No, guys, cast the net on the right side of the boat." I wouldn't want to base my next meal on their fishing success. "Oh, it's tax time? Well, go down to the water and take the coin out of the fish's mouth." Who was the provider? It wasn't them. Secondly, it's obvious they weren't there for Jesus' *protection*. They fled when He was arrested. Peter alone was able to get his sword out of the sheath and cut off the servant's ear, only to watch in amazement as Jesus picked it up and put it back on. Thirdly, they weren't good at *promotion*. On one occasion, Jesus sent them ahead to announce His impending arrival and the Samaritans said, "We don't want Him here." They came running back to Jesus, and they said, "Jesus, they are rejecting You down there. They don't want You to come. Let's call down fire from heaven on them." Jesus said, "You don't know what spirit you are of. I didn't come to destroy lives. I came to save lives." Obviously, they didn't excel at public relations either. On another occasion, some children tried to come to Jesus, and they pushed the little ones away. How did Jesus make it with a crew like His disciples?

I believe certain things are intentionally recorded in Scripture to help us understand what touched the heart of God and caught the eye of Jesus, such that He knew these men "had what it takes" to answer His call and change the world. In seeing that, I encourage you to realize that God is looking for exactly the same things in our lives today. He isn't moved by the things that move the minds and the hearts of men. God is moved by things that have eternal significance and eternal consequence, and in seeing that, we can understand what He is looking for in our lives.

How do I know when I am moving in the unfeigned love of God? How do I know when the unfeigned love of God is touching someone in the world or touching someone in the church through my life? There is a cry in my heart, and perhaps in yours as well, to see that same kind of anointing and empowerment that these inner circle apostles experienced. How long has it been since your shadow healed anyone? How long has it been since you raised anyone from the dead? Some may say, "That was for them, not for us." Show me that in Scripture! That is for the church. That is for us. That is for this generation. Now is the day of salvation. The word "salvation" comes from the Greek word "*sozo*,", and it means "the whole provision of God for the whole man; spirit, soul, and body." Healing, liberty, victory, empowerment, and anointing...now!

Let's consider what it was about Peter, James, and John that caught Jesus' attention.

Net Casters

Matthew 4:18 states, "And Jesus, walking by the Sea of Galilee, saw." The Holy Spirit records what Jesus *saw* because it's important to God. It has everything to do with His selection of these men. It doesn't say He saw that they were tall or handsome. It doesn't say He saw that they had religious credentials. It doesn't say He saw that they were highly educated. It doesn't say He saw that they were strong and eloquent of speech. He "saw two brethren, Simon called Peter, and Andrew his brother casting a net into the sea." He *saw them casting a net* into the sea, and immediately He turned to them and said, "Follow Me."

We can conclude that it was significant to Jesus when He saw these men casting their nets. A net is a device which is used to catch fish. Jesus wasn't moved by the fact that they owned a net. He wasn't moved by them comparing their net with someone else's net. He wasn't even moved by the age or appearance of the net. He was moved by the fact that they were casting what they had. They were not ashamed to cast what they had. They didn't take their net and advertise it, nor did they take their net and display it so that when Jesus walked by they could say, "Jesus, isn't this a lovely net?" No. They were net casters. They were active. They were there to catch fish.

We have a concept in the church world that there are certain people who are hired and paid to win souls. Some people may say, "I will pray for you, Pastor, because you are not winning many souls anymore." God wants to remind you and me that we _all_ have a net. Some Christians may say, "I haven't been to Bible school. I don't have credentials." Jesus didn't ask these men for their fishing credentials. He didn't ask them how successful they were. He was looking for people to carry the unfeigned love of God to a lost generation, people that were committed to casting their net. Likewise, I believe that God is calling every believer to become personally and actively involved by faithfully casting our net daily wherever we find ourselves. You may say, "But I cast and I don't get very many fish." Just keep casting. Don't be impressed or depressed by the number of fish in your net. Just be faithful to continually cast your net, because Jesus is pleased with net casters.

Jesus said in Mark 8:38, "Whosoever is ashamed of Me and My words in this adulterous and sinful generation, of him also will I be ashamed when I come in the glory of My Father and with the holy angels." I believe that the Holy Spirit wants to bring boldness to the people of God. Every one of us has been strategically placed in this world, not only in the place where we live, but also where we work. We must be faithful to cast our net in the place where we are.

I want to call your attention to the fact that fishing with a net is different than fishing with lures or with live bait. There are certain lures that attract only certain kinds of fish. You might say, "Well, I am only looking for a particular kind of fish." But Jesus is looking for net casters. We must lay down every prejudice and reach out to everyone, regardless of age, race, gender, or social standing. All are welcome in the family of God. That is the heart of Jesus.

Cast Your Own Net

Simon Peter, this same man that Jesus saw casting the net, authored II Peter 3:9, which declares that the Lord "is not willing that any should perish, but that all should come to the knowledge of repentance." Peter didn't start out understanding that truth. He had a vision of a sheet (Acts 10), the four corners that came down containing clean and unclean beasts, and the voice of God spoke and said, "Peter, rise and eat." Peter said, "Oh, no, I won't do that. I am a sanctified religious man. I don't eat anything unclean." God said, "Peter, don't call anything unclean or common that I call clean. Don't get picky and choosy." Peter didn't even receive it the first time. God had to preach the same sermon to him three times until he finally said, "Oh, I get it. I am supposed to just cast out my net and let You fill it, God."

Jesus saw them casting *their own* nets, not someone else's. Sometimes we say, "Lord, if I could only sing like that person or preach like that person or teach like that one, I would cast out my net." However, we are not called to cast out someone else's net. We are called to cast out our own net. I look at my net next to others' nets, and I am not impressed with mine. But Jesus didn't ask me to be impressed with my net. He asked me simply to cast it. We don't want to be like the man that hid his talent, then someday stand before Jesus and say, "Jesus, look at my net. It's folded neatly and it has not been soiled. It is just like new, Jesus. I have really protected it." You must cast your net out every day wherever you are. You may be surprised by what you may find flopping around in there. You might even say, "Wow, I never thought God would get that one."

God puts the fish in the net. Your responsibility is to cast it out. You may say, "I am not a good talker. I don't know if I could lead anyone to Christ." Just give them your testimony. Tell them Jesus loves them. People need to hear that message.

Mending the Nets

Matthew 4:21 declares, "And going on from thence, He saw other two brethren. And these two were James, the son of Zebedee, and John his brother, and they were in a ship, and they were with Zebedee their father, and they were mending their nets." Jesus is not only interested in the net casters; He is interested in the net menders. In the process of casting, because of the irregularity of the sea bottom and the many objects that are on the bottom or floating, nets can get torn. A good fisherman knows that he will catch far fewer fish in a torn net than a mended one.

We must understand something about the heart of God that motivated Jesus as He healed the sick, raised the dead, changed the lives of people, and set the captives free. He didn't see them in their filth and failure. He saw them in their woundedness. He saw them as torn, hurting people. Peter was one of them. Jesus said, "Thou art, but thou shalt be." "Peter, you have some rough edges, but I don't see you as torn and useless. I don't see you as a failure. I am the great mender. Where is the needle and thread?" Jesus came to heal the broken hearted. In Luke 4:18-19, Jesus quoted Isaiah 61:1-3 and said, "I conduct a divine exchange program. If you bring Me ashes, I will give you beauty." That is a good deal for us. Ashes are all that remains of something that once was beautiful, strong, and functional. Our human tendency is to throw the ashes away. Jesus said, "I know ashes don't look like much, but don't throw them away. Give them to Me and I will give you beauty in exchange for them."

"And I will give you the oil of joy for mourning. And I will give you the garment of praise for the spirit of heaviness, because," He says, "I am a net mender." Isaiah 61:1 in essence states, "The Spirit of the Lord is upon me for He hath anointed me to mend nets." A big problem is failing to see ourselves as nets that need mended. We deceive ourselves by thinking that because of our good works or our church membership, we are all right. No. My friend, you are a torn net. I am a torn net. Jesus takes that which most people would discard, and He reaches for the needle and thread.

When my grandson was three years old, he had the mentality of this generation. When something didn't work, he said, "Buy new one." "Buy new one, Papa." That is what we do today, right? We don't fix things. We throw them away and buy another one. When I was young, my dad used to spend hours working on his old 1934 Ford. It was all we had. When something broke, we fixed it. We couldn't afford to buy a new one. I am not downplaying the blessing that God gives. I am not saying that we are worse off because we are living in today's world. I am simply saying that there is a mentality of "discard this and get something better." That is not the mentality of Jesus. Sometimes, as we are working with people, praying for people, and trying our best to reach people, we can see their brokenness and all of the holes in their net, and we can be tempted to say, "I will forget about that one. They are never going to be mended anyway. I will go get a better candidate." Jesus is saying to us, "Listen, I am looking for net menders." The world desperately needs net menders. We don't have to tell people that they are sinners. We don't have to tell them they have missed the mark. We don't have to tell them they are headed for a Godless eternity. They need someone that will mend their torn net, someone that will help them.

Jesus' Needle and Thread

Undoubtedly, every one of us could say that there were times when the Lord took His needle and thread—perhaps through a friend, a sermon, a song, or a church service—and mended us.

When one of my sons was very young, he had a talent for breaking things. We used to laugh because no matter what he broke, he had the concept that Dad could fix it. He would come to me with the pieces and he would say, "Daddy, 'fits' it. 'Fits' it." The Lord revealed to me that that is really our ministry as believers. When He causes people to cross our path and they begin to pour out their heart to us, what they are really saying is, "'Fits' it. Will someone 'fits' it?" Jesus is saying that He is looking for people that want to fix it. If you use the needle you have, He will give you a bigger one. Don't sit back and say, "I am not good enough." Start using what you have.

Jesus saw men that wouldn't throw away what others would have thrown away. He said, "That is who I want, because in the next three and a half years, I am going to encounter multitudes of broken people. I want men that won't throw them away but will receive them and love them and help them." That is unfeigned love. That is what Jesus had. People said, "Jesus, what are You doing eating with the publicans and sinners?" He said, "I am fixing them." "Jesus, we don't understand Your ministry. You don't look and act like others." He simply went around fixing people.

Acts 10:38 declares that "God anointed Jesus of Nazareth who went about doing good and healing all that were oppressed of the devil." God filled us with the Holy Ghost so we could find broken nets and mend them. He will give us the proper needle and thread for the task. Jesus said, "That is the kind of people I want. Net menders."

Washing the Nets

There is one more thing that Scripture declares that Jesus saw. It is found in Luke's account of the same event, and rather than the word "saw" being specifically written, it's there by implication. Luke 5:1-2 states, "And it came to pass that as the people pressed upon Him to hear the Word of God, He stood by the lake of Gennesaret, and saw two ships standing by the lake, but the fishermen were gone out of them." Why were they gone out of them? "They were washing their nets." Who were they? Please note verse 10. "And so also James and John, the sons of Zebedee, which were partners with Simon. And Jesus said unto them, Fear not, from henceforth thou shalt catch men." They are not only net casters and net menders, but they are also net washers. Three verbs: casting, mending, and washing. Three men: Peter, James, and John.

Why do you need to wash nets? Because in the process of fishing, as you cast the net and drag it through the water to bring it in, you not only pick up fish, but you pick up the contaminants from that particular area. They may be rocks, weeds, stones, twigs, or garbage. If we don't wash our net, our effectiveness to cast it again and bring in more fish will be hindered. Our net is going to get heavy, and these kinds of objects will disturb the water such that the fish will be frightened and swim away. We can only be effective and receptive to the fish God wants to send if all of the garbage and junk is washed from our net.

One of the devil's most devious and effective devices is to fill our net with junk. Some may say, "I would get involved, but I was really offended by brother so and so or sister so and so, and they did this and they did that and they did something else." You are letting your net get full of stones. My heart breaks because I see people in the church world that have the talent, skill, ability, and calling to be effective, mighty people of God, yet they have allowed themselves to become ineffective. They are doing nothing. Their chin is touching the ground and their nose is running. They are always complaining about something. We need to have some net-washing services!

Let's get the junk out. Every day I have to wash my net. We need to be clean and free to be able to serve God. I don't care who caused it, and I don't care who said what to whom. The issue is this: is your net clean? Forgiveness is vital to functioning in the anointing and being effective in ministry.

Jesus saw Peter, James, and John washing their nets. They were getting all of the junk out, the sticks and the stones. Jesus saw them washing _their_ nets, not someone else's nets. After they had washed their nets, Jesus sent them out into the deep, and filled the nets with so many fish that they needed the help of other boats to bring them all in.

What Catches the Attention of Jesus?

I believe that the Holy Spirit included these scriptures to help us understand the actions that caught the attention of Jesus. These disciples were normal people who simply cast their nets, mended their nets, and washed their nets. Jesus effectively said, "You guys are My kind of guys. Come with Me. We are going to change the world, because you understand what is really important. You understand what captures the eye of the Father. You understand. Come follow Me. We are going to turn the world upside down, because you understand unfeigned love toward the brethren." Like Paul said to the church at Corinth, regardless of what you are going through, whether it is affliction, trial, or other difficulty, the unfeigned love of God should still be evident in your life.

We all want and need the unfeigned love of God _to_ us, but if we hear the heart of God, we will understand that His purpose includes the unfeigned love of God working *through* us. Don't let the devil tell you that you're not capable, not chosen, or not part of the plan. You may say, "It doesn't seem to me that I have been very effective." Search your heart. Have you been mending and washing your net? Have you been walking in forgiveness and repentance? Have you made sure that contaminants are out of your net?

The Holy Spirit said, "Write it down, Matthew. Write it down, Luke. Write down what caught My eye. People that are committed to casting, mending, and washing the nets I gave them. These are the kind of people that can carry My unfeigned love to the world."

Chapter 7

Restoring The Fallen

In this chapter, I want to continue to look at God's desire to show His unfeigned love through us. He gives it *to* us that it might flow *through* us. His love doesn't end with our reception of it. His purpose doesn't end with us knowing about it. We are touched that we might touch. We are comforted, not so that we will simply be comfortable, but so that we might comfort others. We are healed that we might heal. We are liberated that we might liberate. We are saved that we might reach the unsaved. You see, God's purpose comes _to_ us that it might be manifest _through_ us. Unless we understand that, we can make the serious mistake of becoming self-centered and self-serving.

In Matthew 10:8, Jesus said, "Freely you have received, freely give." Please take note that there is no period after the word "received." Neither does it read "Freely you have received, so praise Him forevermore." It reads "Freely you have received, [therefore] freely give." We are to be channels and vessels. We are to be people through whom He accomplishes His purposes.

II Corinthians 6 and I Peter 1 both speak of the unfeigned love of God working *through* us. II Corinthians 6:4 declares, "In all things demonstrating ourselves as ministers of God, by love unfeigned." That is how it's demonstrated and identified. As love unfeigned flows through you, it is the evidence that you are a servant of the Lord Jesus Christ. It is recorded in I Peter 1:22 that there needs to be "unfeigned love for the brethren."

Genuine, real love. Lord, help us to understand that, so we don't just go through vain motions and actions.

The Heart of God

It is possible for us to somewhat understand the things of God, the acts of God, and even the ways of God, yet not understand the _heart_ of God. My prayer has always been, "God, show me Your heart. I want to have Your heart." I was fortunate to be raised in church. I was blessed as a young boy to be exposed to the Word of God and the power of God. I know how to "do church," but I want more. I want to know the heart of God. I want to know what He is saying and feeling. I want to know how He is moving and what He wants done. That was the key to the effectiveness of the earthly ministry of Jesus. He said, "I just do what I see the Father do," which implies that He could see the Father, feel the Father, and know what the heart of the Father was. We need that, because otherwise we can make the serious mistake of simply doing good things or doing our own thing, yet not being completely obedient to Him. Obedience is doing His will. That is my heart's cry and my desire.

The book of Acts informs us that Paul went on three missionary journeys and then made a final trip to Rome. In those journeys, we can see the heart of God for the church and for the world. He is saying to us, "If you examine and consider this, you will understand what I am expecting from My people, both individually and collectively in this day." Paul's third missionary journey encompasses Acts chapters 18 through 21. There were great and glorious things that were accomplished through Paul the Apostle as his ministry was drawing to a close. One of the greatest confrontations with the powers of darkness recorded in Scripture is when Paul went to Ephesus and ministered to people who worshipped the goddess Diana. He confronted the worshippers of idols, and the power of God moved so mightily that they brought their idols and destroyed them in a big bonfire, giving glory to God. Then he called all the elders from Ephesus that he might commit unto them the responsibility of overseeing the church. His address to the Ephesian elders (Acts 20:17-38) contains much good advice for church leadership.

The Story of Eutychus

One of the final and glorious miracles that happened on Paul's third missionary journey reveals the heart of God to us. Acts 20:7-12 states, "And upon the first day of the week when the disciples came together Paul preached unto them, ready to depart on the morrow, and continued his speech until midnight. There were many lights in the upper chamber where they were gathered together." Every word in Scripture is significant, so let's continue carefully, "And there sat in a window a certain young man named Eutychus, being fallen into a deep sleep, as Paul was long preaching, he sunk down with sleep and fell down from the third loft and was taken up dead." Another translation adds the phrase "with a broken neck." "And Paul went down and fell on him." This man *sunk* down, then *fell* down, and then Paul *went* down and fell on him, embraced him, and said, "Trouble not yourselves, for his life is in him. And when he therefore was come up again and had broken bread and eaten and talked a long while, even until the break of day. So he departed, and they brought the young man alive and were not a little comforted." They were excited and joyful.

Throughout Scripture, God consistently communicates His truths and holds nothing back. He doesn't interrupt certain passages to apologize. He doesn't say, "I am sorry to have to tell you this, but I must tell you." God isn't embarrassed. God tells it exactly like it is because human nature hasn't changed in two thousand years. We still show remarkable evidence that we are the seed of Adam. Clearly, we all came from the "Adam's family."

Restoration

The unfolding of this miracle unveils, reveals, illuminates, and displays the heart of God to us. Unquestionably, the heart of God is "restoration." Restoration sometimes involves resurrection. Restoration is very important, because unless we are restored, we can't be a part of what God is doing. Restoration is necessary because we live in a world in which iniquity abounds, and there is the ever present danger of falling, perhaps even multiple times. Regardless of how many times we fall, the solution is to be restored back to God.

There was something going on in that upper room that Eutychus ceased to be a part of. He was no longer there, no longer "tuned in," no longer involved. He hadn't committed any great sin. He hadn't purposely decided that he was going to have no part in the things of God or have nothing to do with what God was all about. It simply says that he fell. He just slipped.

The prophet Joel prophesied about the end times. In Joel 2:25, in the last days, God declares "I will restore unto you the years that the locust hath eaten, the cankerworm, the caterpillar, and the palmerworm, My great army which I sent among you." I want to put the emphasis on "restore." God is saying, "One of the things I am going to do in the last hour is restore everything that needs restoration."

The revival fire of God is going to be so evident in the last days, it is going to awaken and quicken and startle. It is going to shake everything that can be shaken. There will be a day of judgment, to be certain. But the heart of God today is to restore.

I want to be restored, and I want to be a restorer, because that's the heart of God. I believe that if every person who ever confessed Jesus as Lord or has been a part of a church turned back to God, there would not be enough churches to contain all the people. There are many that need to be restored.

A Fortunate Man in the Light

Let us consider more closely the scene on that Sunday night nearly two thousand years ago. Acts 20:8 states that there were *many lights* in the room. The word "lights" refers to lamps of oil that were burning, providing both light and heat.

Inside the room there was an abundance of light, and the Word of God was being taught by the Apostle Paul. The oil in the lamps represents the Holy Spirit and the anointing.

The Word of God was being spoken and the room was filled with light. One of the listeners sat in a window. In those days, most windows were just openings in the wall. This man, by positioning himself in the window, was exposing himself to two opposite environments. It was midnight and therefore it was dark outside, a stark contrast to the many lights inside. On one side was light, and on the other side was darkness. Also, because he was in the window, he could hear the Word of God on one side, and on the other side he could hear the street noises, the noises of the world.

This man in the window was exposed to two differing environments, both of which were contending for his attention and commitment. His name was Eutychus. The Bible never gives us a name of a place or a name of a person unless it's important. The word "Eutychus" by definition means "the happy one" or "the fortunate one." That is a good description of a believer, a Christian. We are fortunate to belong to Jesus. We are fortunate to be born again. We are fortunate to be headed for a glorious eternity with God. We are fortunate to be free of our sins and our iniquity. If you never have a big bank account, drive a big car, or live in a big house, it doesn't matter. You are very fortunate if you belong to Jesus.

He was not only fortunate, but he was happy. He was a happy believer. He knew the provision of God, the joy of the Lord, the goodness of the Lord, and the blessing of the Lord, because names in that day were representative of the nature or the character of the individual that bore them. In Eutychus, I see someone who has been touched by God and blessed of God. He was a part of the church, of the Body of Christ. He could have been doing something else that Sunday evening, but he chose to attend the gathering of the believers.

Compromise

Though Eutychus was apparently a happy and fortunate believer, he had placed himself in a position of apparent compromise. As he sat there in the window, "half in and half out" of the room, he was exposed to both light and darkness, and exposed to both the Word of God and the noise of the streets.

The Christian life would be easier if, having been exposed to the light, we were never confronted again with the dark, and once having heard the Word of God we would be deafened to contrary voices. There are many voices, not only from the enemy, but also from our flesh, that vie for our attention. We are constantly exposed to these *other* noises. It's important that we make choices that are consistent with pleasing God. Eutychus failed to do that. He was not only listening to the Word of God; he was listening to other voices as well. Like Eutychus, if we are not careful, we can make the mistake of listening to other voices, such as the voices of criticism, cynicism, and complaint. If we are listening to the wrong voices, we are compromising our relationship with God. Each of us must make a choice and take a stand, saying, "I am only going to listen to the Word of God. I am going to listen to what God has to say."

Eutychus was sitting in the window between light and darkness, between the Word of God and street noise, trying to maintain his balance. It reminds me of an experience I had when I was standing on a dock and stepped with one leg into a boat that wasn't tied to the dock. The boat was moving one way, and the dock was not moving at all. Welcome to the world of the falling!

The Process: Slumping, Then Falling

Eutychus was sitting there, listening to Paul preach. Granted, Paul was preaching a long time. It was midnight, and he hadn't finished. The Bible describes Eutychus' regression. It doesn't say, "All of a sudden, he fell" or that someone pushed him. It says first he *slumped* down, and then he *fell* down. Have you ever fallen asleep when you wanted to stay awake?

The process of descending into sleep is worthy of note. From the state of hearing words and understanding them clearly, you descend to the state of hearing words but failing to understand the meaning. As the descent continues, you no longer hear distinguishable words, only noises. You know someone is talking but you have no idea, nor even care to know, what they are saying. In the final descent, you no longer even hear noises. This is a normal and totally acceptable process in the physical realm of a person's life. This is how we "fall" asleep.

However, it is an unwelcome and devastating process in the spiritual realm of a person's life. Can such a thing happen? Jesus said that it can. In chapters 2 and 3 of the book of Revelation, He is quoted as cautioning the church seven times about such a possibility. He said: "He that hath ears to hear, let him hear what the Spirit saith to the churches." To hear the Word of God without impact, conviction, or change, is a sad and potentially devastating thing.

Eutychus, our happy brother, had slumped into total sleep. The only thing remaining after you *slump* down is to *fall* down. I want to be so sensitive that if I see people spiritually slumping, I want to go to them, talk to them, and pray for them. I don't want to wait until they fall.

Paul Shows the Heart of God

Paul had reason to react differently than he did. Paul could have become offended about the whole thing. He could have said, "I don't come here very often. It's been a long time since I have been here, and I will likely never be here again. I am tired, weary, and I've been teaching and preaching for hours, giving everything I have, and Eutychus falls asleep on me and then literally falls. I guess that serves him right." Paul could also have simply concluded, "We didn't need him anyway." The room is already full. What does one listener matter?

Be reminded that the heart of Jesus was so touched with the one lost sheep that He left the other ninety nine sheep to search for the one that was lost (Luke 15:4). I see the same heart in Paul. I don't know how many people were in the room listening to him teach, but he cared about the one man that fell asleep while he was teaching. He cared about the one who chose to sit in the window and who eventually fell. Please see the heart of God manifest through Paul.

This condition of slumbering and falling is an example of the spiritual condition in our world today. Jesus said these words, recorded in Matthew 24:12, "Because iniquity shall abound, the love of many shall wax cold." Another translation says "grow cold" and another says "cool off." Because the darkness is so strong, the light can begin to fade out. In II Thessalonians 2:3, Paul states, "Let no man deceive you by any means before that day come." He is speaking of the coming of the Lord. Before Jesus comes again, he stated, "There shall come a *falling away* first."

In II Timothy 3:1 Paul declares, "This know, In the last days, perilous times shall come." It's interesting that he didn't speak of nuclear warfare or bacteriological warfare when referring to perilous times. Instead, he spoke of the condition of the hearts of men. Paul declared, "Men shall be lovers of their own selves, trucebreakers, incontinent." Verse 5 states, "Having a form of godliness, but denying the power thereof." The word "denying" in another translation is the word "*forsaking*." It doesn't mean denying in the sense of saying "I don't believe it's true." It means denying in the sense of "walking away from something that you once had." Listen to those verbal expressions: "cool off," "fall away," and "forsake." Staying on fire for God is not easy. We must work at it. Many distractions from the world are undoubtedly going to come against us.

Eutychus lay outside on the ground with a broken neck. The Apostle Paul, not offended, not forsaking the brother, reminds me of what he wrote in Galatians 6:1. Paul not only wrote this, but he lived it. He said, "Brethren, if a man be overtaken in a fault ye which are spiritual restore such a one in the spirit of meekness." This is the Bible definition of what it means to be spiritual. It isn't defined by seniority or by how many songs we can sing or how many Scriptures we can quote. It is defined by the condition of our heart. God said if you are spiritual, you will be a restorer.

"Restore such a one in the spirit of meekness." You don't run down to the man lying there with a broken neck and say, "I told you not to sit in the window. I knew that was going to happen." That is not "in the spirit of meekness." Paul goes on to say, "Considering yourself, lest you also be tempted." He is saying that every one of us have the potential of slumbering, slipping, and falling. Remember that when you are ministering restoration. Don't look _down_, look _across_. Don't hit him on the head, give him a helping hand. Don't run around telling everyone what he did wrong. Take it to Jesus. Fall on your face at the foot of the cross and pray about it.

Paul Went Down to Him

"Considering yourself, lest you also be tempted." The Apostle Paul had a brother who was overtaken in a fault, who fell asleep and had fallen because he didn't pay attention. What is the first thing Paul did? He _went down to the fallen one_. This demonstrates the heart of God toward a fallen one. Paul could have acted "super spiritual," leaned out of the window high above Eutychus, and said, "Dear brother, in the name of Jesus, get back up here." However, God is showing us, through Paul's actions, that there comes a time when we must go down to the fallen one and meet him right where he or she is.

We must feel what they feel and hurt as they hurt. Paul went down to where Eutychus was. He was effectively saying, "I am not too great or too important to go down to the fallen one." We aren't told how he interrupted or suspended his teaching after Eutychus fell. Paul might have said, "Folks, please bear with me for a moment. I will be right back. I must bring one of our members back." Sometimes the Holy Spirit interrupts a gathering to reach out to just one person.

Paul Fell On Him

Paul went down to Eutychus, and then he _fell on him_. He not only went to where Eutychus was, but he also identified with his condition. After someone has fallen three floors and is lying there with a broken neck, he is undoubtedly an unpleasant sight. Paul wasn't afraid to identify himself with this broken man. The life that was in Paul was beginning to be communicated into that man. The death in the man was not coming into Paul, but the life in Paul was going into the dead man. Life is greater than death. Light is greater than darkness. "The light shineth in darkness and the darkness comprehended it not." (John 1:5). Paul fell on him, and in doing so, he was effectively saying, "Eutychus, I care about you. God put you here with us, and we need you."

Paul Embraced Him

The third thing Paul did was embrace Eutychus. He went down to him, he fell on him, and he *embraced* him. The word "embraced" means "to have compassion and to intercede for." There are times when you simply command, "In the name of Jesus, rise and walk," like Peter and John did going into the temple (Acts 3:6). There are other times when you embrace the fallen and hold them until the life that is in you flows into them.

Embracing someone is often more challenging than commanding them. There may be times the Lord lets us command, but there are also going to be times when He calls us to embrace. Paul was embracing the person with whom he had a right to be offended. Can you imagine the atmosphere in that upper room when Paul came walking back in, not to have a funeral, but with a spring in his step, joy in his heart, and Eutychus at his side? Perhaps he said, "Now we can go on with the teaching. Our brother has been restored." Can you see the heart of God in this? I am speaking of unfeigned love toward the brethren, you who are servants, ministering unfeigned love. The cry of my heart is that God will so fill me with that kind of love that He can restore the fallen through me.

God Can Keep Us from Falling

The good news is that it isn't necessary for us to fall. Jude 24 declares, "Unto Him that is able to keep us from falling and to present us faultless before His throne with exceeding great joy." God keeps us from falling by getting our attention when we begin to slump. When we start slumping, He nudges us gently or takes more aggressive action, depending on what is needed to "wake us up" and therefore keep us from falling. We may say, "God, quit picking on me." He says, "I love you too much to let you slump and fall. I will deal with you while you are slumping so that we can prevent the fall. I want you to sit up straight and get serious about our relationship. Shake off everything that is slowing you down." Hebrews 12:1 declares, "Wherefore seeing we also are compassed about with so great a cloud of witnesses, let us lay aside every weight, and the sin which doth so easily beset us, and let us run with patience the race that is set before us." It declares, "Let us lay aside every weight." The weights are the things that make us slump. I decided many years ago that I cannot afford to carry the weight of unforgiveness or criticism in my heart. I need the anointing too badly.

It is time for us to realize that God is in the restoring business. He is awakening and anointing His church because our world is filled with people that have fallen. Some people who once praised God, studied their Bible, and worshipped Him, are walking in darkness today. They have fallen, but God loves them and wants them restored. Lord, let us be an oasis in the desert, a place where the weak, weary, broken, and blind can come and find life and love, and be restored. Lord, help us to embrace and bring back into the fold those who have slumped and fallen. We want to have Your heart for the fallen. We want to be dispensers of Your unfeigned love.

1395602

Made in the USA